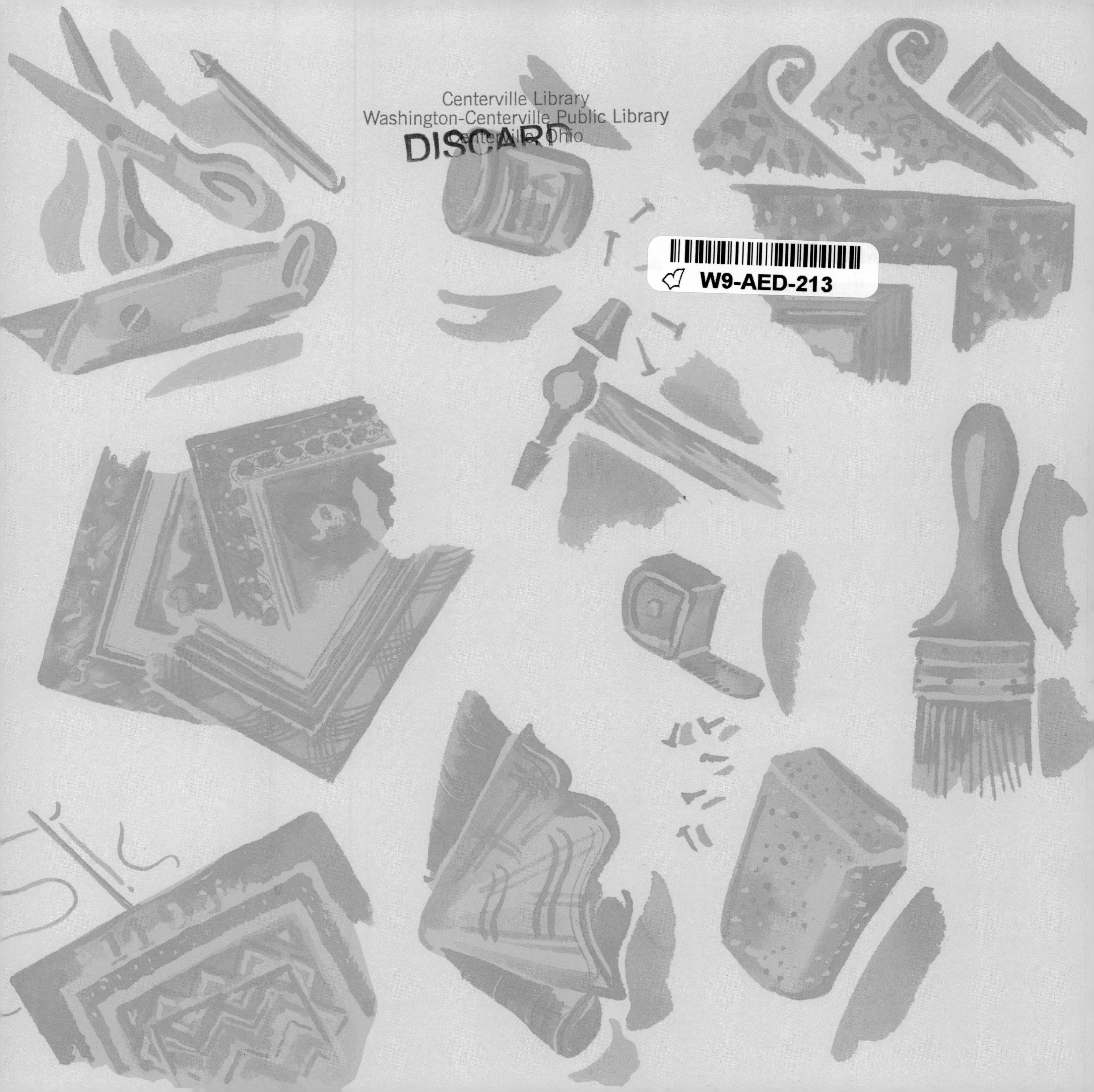

# PICTURE FRAMING

O nata lux de lumine

*Lesu redemptor sacculi*

Dignare clemens supplicum

Laudes precesque sumere.

WB

# New Crafts
# Picture Framing

### Rian Kanduth

### Photography by Nicki Dowey

### LORENZ BOOKS

This edition first published in 1999 by
Lorenz Books

Lorenz Books is an imprint of
Anness Publishing Limited
Hermes House
88–89 Blackfriars Road
London SE1 8HA

This edition is distributed in Canada by
Raincoast Books Distribution Limited.

ISBN 0 7548 0189 6

A CIP catalogue record for this book
is available from the British Library.

Publisher: Joanna Lorenz
Senior Editor: Doreen Palamartschuk
Designer: Lilian Lindblom
Photographer: Nicki Dowey
Illustrators: Madeleine David,
    Vana Haggerty and Robert Highton

Printed in Hong Kong/China

10 9 8 7 6 5 4 3 2 1

# CONTENTS

| | |
|---|---|
| INTRODUCTION | 7 |
| ORIGINS OF THE FRAME | 8 |
| GALLERY | 12 |
| MATERIALS | 18 |
| EQUIPMENT | 20 |
| BASIC TECHNIQUES | 22 |
| DECORATIVE WINDOW MOUNT | 34 |
| STEPPED WINDOW MOUNT | 36 |
| VELVET-COVERED MOUNT | 38 |
| MULTIPLE WINDOW MOUNT | 41 |
| LIME-WAXED FRAME | 44 |
| COLOURWASHED FRAME | 46 |
| WOODSTAINED FRAME | 48 |
| CRAQUELURE FRAME | 50 |
| SCORCHED FRAME | 52 |
| RAISED MOTIF FRAME | 54 |
| FRAMED STONE | 56 |
| METAL FOIL FRAME | 58 |
| DECOUPAGE FRAME | 61 |
| LEAD FRAME | 64 |
| OIL-GILDED FRAME | 68 |
| VERRE EGLOMISÉ MIRROR | 70 |
| FRAMING A CANVAS | 73 |
| FRAMING A TEXTILE | 76 |
| BIRCH PLYWOOD FRAME | 79 |
| RECLAIMED TIMBER FRAME | 82 |
| PENWORK FRAME | 84 |
| TORTOISESHELL FRAME | 86 |
| EMILY'S FRAME | 90 |
| TEMPLATES | 94 |
| SUPPLIERS & ACKNOWLEDGEMENTS | 95 |
| INDEX | 96 |

# INTRODUCTION

PICTURE FRAMES CAN BE AS EYE-CATCHING AND INTERESTING AS THE WORK THEY ADORN. AN IMAGINATIVE WELL-MADE SURROUND CAN ENHANCE ANY IMAGE, BE IT A PICTURE, PHOTOGRAPH, TEXTILE OR LESS CONVENTIONAL ARTWORK, AND THROUGHOUT HISTORY, STYLES OF FRAMES HAVE OFTEN REFLECTED TRENDS IN ART OF THE ERA. MAKING AND DECORATING PICTURE FRAMES IS A REWARDING AND CHALLENGING CRAFT, AND CAN BE MASTERED QUICKLY AND SUCCESSFULLY WITH A FEW BASIC CARPENTRY TECHNIQUES THAT GUARANTEE PROFESSIONAL-LOOKING RESULTS. WITH THE VAST ARRAY OF PRE-CUT WOODEN MOULDINGS AND MOUNTBOARDS AVAILABLE, THE CHOICE OF WHICH STYLE OF FRAME YOU CAN MAKE IS ENDLESS. THERE ARE ALSO MANY PRE-DECORATED MOULDINGS ON THE MARKET TODAY, BUT OFTEN IT IS MORE ENJOYABLE EXPERIMENTING, DEVISING AND DECORATING YOUR OWN INDIVIDUAL FRAME.

*Left: Frames with metallic finishes can be made by many different methods, for example gilding, using metal paints or decorating with metal objects.*

# ORIGINS OF THE FRAME

THROUGHOUT HISTORY PICTURE FRAMES HAVE BEEN AN INTEGRAL PART OF EVERY HOUSEHOLD'S INVENTORY. YET THE FRAME IS A CURIOUS OBJECT THAT IS USUALLY OVERLOOKED IN THE STUDY OF ART. PICTURE FRAMING IS A SKILFUL CRAFT WHICH HAS BEEN IN EXISTENCE FOR HUNDREDS OF YEARS. IT IS PRIMARILY CONCERNED WITH THE PROTECTION AND PRESERVATION OF ARTWORKS BUT IT ALSO SERVES AS A MEANS OF DISPLAYING PICTURES.

"A good picture deserves a good frame and a bad picture may sometimes preserve its place longer by having a handsome frame" (Charles Willson Peal c.1807).

Frames surrounding images have been an integral part of Western art since early Roman times and many Christian Byzantine mosaics had patterned borders.

In the Medieval period, during the 11th and 12th centuries, the frame was drawn as part of the picture. Monks added illuminated borders to their decorated manuscripts. Although such "frames" were clearly separate from the text itself, the lettering used for the text often included aspects of the border design. Giotto's frescoes in Florence and Assisi had borders painted around them to separate scenes.

The first recorded wooden frames appeared during the 13th century, found in churches and cathedrals. They were designed by craftsmen who also created screens, pulpits and choirstalls. These frames often took the form of a "triptych" – three panels of wood hinged together; the central panel held the main painting and the two side panels contained a design or painting complementary to it.

The paintings of this period were usually ecclesiastical and of icons or saints. The surrounding frame generally included elements of architecture. One popular

*Above: The Virgin Mary between two angels. A 13th-century painting and frame from Siena, Italy.*

*Above: Jesus Christ on the cross and in six scenes of the Passion. Painted c.1475 by Maître François, École de Fouquet, from a French manuscript.*

*Above: The Last Judgement triptych by Hieronymus Bosch, 1450–1516.*

style during the 13th century was the "tabernacle" frame, which incorporated pilasters and half columns.

During the 15th century, the Renaissance in Italy brought great changes in art and framing: as well as ecclesiastical paintings, wealthy patrons began to commission artists to execute portraits. Artists themselves were now beginning to recognize the frame as an important element in the pictures they were creating. As artists became more respected, they had less time to make their own frames, so this role frequently passed to furniture and cabinet makers. In this way, the separate craft of picture framing slowly emerged.

The changes that began in Italy spread to other parts of Europe. However, each country developed its own particular features. Germany concentrated on carving dense, crisp decoration, often ornamented with ivory inlays, shells,

copper and semi-precious stones. Spain adopted a stronger, simpler, heavier ornamentation, and used a very dark tone for its gold leaf. Frames were now starting to take on a style inspired by ancient Greek architecture. As time progressed Italian frames became more elaborately carved and gilded.

During the 16th century, the focus of the arts was now switching from Italy to France, where Francis I (1515–47) invited Italian craftsmen and artists to Court. In England, the reign of Henry VIII (1509–47) also brought many foreign craftsmen as demand grew for paintings and frames, both for the great palace collections of the King and in private homes. After the Dissolution of the Monasteries, craftsmen went into secular service and found a market for their skills in private homes. There was an ongoing battle between Henry VIII and Francis, as each attempted

*Above: Two carved, pierced and gilded Rococo frames from the 18th century decorated with shell themes, and in the centre, a faux tortoiseshell frame with ebony.*

*Above: Four 14th-century Spanish frames. Left to right: a frame painted flat with a deeply cut scrolled corner orna-ment and a raised inner profile; two gilded drawing frames, one has a marbled fascia to the outer edge and the other a leaf-embellished ogee to the inner; a darkly gilded frame.*

*Above: A late 17th-century design for a mirror frame with mythological figures and allegory by Andrea Brustolon (1662–1732).*

to out-do the other in terms of artistic style and opulence.

The frame became increasingly ornate during the late 17th and 18th centuries, firstly with the highly decorative Baroque style and then in the Rococo style. This reflected the trends in painting and, even more importantly, the decorative arts during the period.

Craftsmen required a great degree of skill to produce these elaborate frames. The popularity of such extravagant styles decreased progressively, and there was a gradual return to simpler, more austere frames. Toward the end of the 18th century, geometric forms again became fashionable. In 1758, the English Adam brothers, visited Italy frequently, returning with detailed studies of ancient Roman and Greek architecture. In spite of the spreading influence of the French, their classical style became a major influence in picture frame making.

*Above: The Archduke Leopold William, Governor of Flanders, in his art gallery, a painting that clearly depicts contemporary styles of frames. Painted by David Teniers II, a Flemish artist (1610–90).*

Dutch frames had their own individual development, especially during the 17th century, although their original inspiration had also been the Italian Renaissance. Dutch artists and framemakers often painted the frames black with very little use of gilding or colouring. Dutch merchant shippers had begun to import ebony and other exotic woods, which inspired framemakers to experiment and use veneers of wood, tortoiseshell and turtleshell.

At the end of the 17th century the influx of the Huguenots in England brought the talent and the influence of their carvers, gilders and cabinetmakers from France. At the same time, rulers William and Mary favoured Dutch designs. Oval frames appeared and were

popularly used for portraits. In 1733 the duty on imported timber was abolished and mahogany became fashionable. One can still find mahogany frames of this period but they are becoming very rare.

Once again, Italy set the style at the end of the 18th century – a more severe style of decoration was in vogue, known as Neo-Classicism, in reaction to the extravagant taste of the previous movements. In France, Louis XVI frames were of a plainer geometric form, frequently rectangular or oval, some surmounted by crowns or wreaths. During the reign of Napoleon Bonaparte, at the beginning of the 19th century, a love of uniformity arose. The "Empire" frame consisted of plaster motifs derived from palm leaves, lotus and papyrus, an Egyptian influence, as well as classic forms.

"Composition" frames were introduced at the start of the 19th century and began to replace the traditional carved wood as a material. Whiting, resin and size (animal glue) were heated, amalgamated and pressed into moulds of boxwood and left to set, and then the ornament was applied to a basic wooden profile. Frames could be produced much quicker and became less

*Above: A portrait of Mademoiselle Desmares, an actress with the Comédie Française. Painted c.1720–30.*

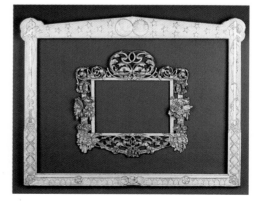

*Above: A composition frame decorated with celestial bosses, and an English 19th-century frame carved, pierced and overpainted in the style of Grinling Gibbons, and decorated with scrolling acanthus leaves, flowers and grapes.*

*Above: Two French Louis XVI carved and gilded oval frames with shot and lamb's tongue ornament to the edges and ribbon-tied crests. The centre frame is a French Louis XVI carved and gilded frame; the ogee knull has a decorative leaf and crest.*

expensive than individually carved frames. In England, during the Victorian period, Rococo imitations were prevalent until the 1880s, when there was a revival of Neo-Classicism and of the Adam brothers' designs. The oval was revived and at the end of the century Art Nouveau appeared with Oriental influences.

In efforts to break from the past, the 20th century has seen many experiments in framing. Presently most frames are quite plain. However, re-creations of the elaborately carved and gilded frames of the past are occasionally seen. Highly skilled wood carvers and gilders still exist, although there are far fewer than in previous times. The history of picture framing, like so much else in history, is cyclical: styles come and go, and return again.

*Above: An early 20th-century French frame with Art Nouveau motifs showing a family portrait.*

# GALLERY

THE FRAME IS OFTEN CONSIDERED TO BE SECONDARY TO THE WORK THAT IT ENCLOSES. HOWEVER, A FRAME, BE IT UNDERSTATED OR ELABORATE, CAN HAVE A HUGE IMPACT — BOTH FAVOURABLE AND UNFORTUNATE — ON THE ARTWORK ITSELF. THE FOLLOWING PAGES SHOW THE DECORATIVE SCOPE EMPLOYED BY CONTEMPORARY FRAMEMAKERS, FROM MINIMALIST OR NATURAL FINISHES TO HIGHLY ORNATE CARVED AND GILDED EXAMPLES.

*Above:* LARGE MANUFACTURED SWEPT FRAME
This frame incorporates silver beading on the rebate and outside edges to complement the dark silver grey face. The moulding is wide and deep, and the aperture for the mirror small.
RIAN KANDUTH

*Left:* LARGE HOCKEY OR HALF-ROUND FRAME
Made of obeche wood, this frame has been decorated with decoupage using old sheet music. The paper was hand-torn and then stained with dilute burnt sienna gouache, before being protected with several coats of shellac.
Frame by RIAN KANDUTH; collection of MAGGIE and DENNIS JAKEMAN

*Above:* SMALL CUT BACK ASH FRAME
This simple frame has a dark grey wood stain finish, protected with several coats of clear wax. Since the ash frame is designed to frame three-dimensional objects, small wooden fillets, painted white, were inserted to prevent the glass touching the artwork.
Artwork and frame by RIAN KANDUTH

*Left:* CROSS-OVER FRAME
The colour of the oak frame was heightened using a dark oak stain. It houses a double-thickness single window mount. This type of mount gives an unusual amount of depth on the bevel, but it is difficult to cut accurately. Frame by RIAN KANDUTH; picture by ANDY KINGSBURY

*Below:* SMALL HOCKEY FRAMES
These pine frames have been water-gilded using an assortment of different gold and white gold leaf. Some of the frames have been distressed with pumice powder. The white gold leaf was left to tarnish for eight months. RIAN KANDUTH

*Right:* LARGE ASH CUSHION FRAME (left) and SMALL FLAT-FACED ASH FRAME
These two natural wood frames were carefully sanded to produce a smooth finish. The flat-faced frame was left untreated, while the cushion frame was finished with several coats of clear wax. RIAN KANDUTH

*Below:* MOSAIC MIRROR
The shape of this simple, but effective frame has arabic influences, with a domed-shaped top. The background of the frame is painted with aquamarine emulsion. Clear safety glass was arranged on the surface and grouted. The colour shows through the glass to create an even mosaic finish.
DEE MORGAN

*Right:* WAVY MOULDING
The pine frame has been stained dark mahogany and contains a black single window mount. The picture itself is extremely small and would be lost in a large mount or a small moulding. With this combination, the frame draws the eye inward to the photograph.
RIAN KANDUTH

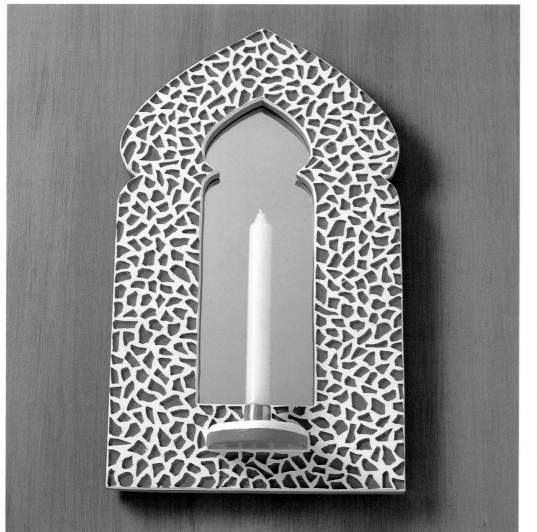

*Above:* SMALL HOCKEY FRAME
This frame was made from ramin, a very straight and close-grained wood, and stained with dilute grey wood stain. A stepped mount breaks up the large area of whiteness surrounding the artwork.
RIAN KANDUTH

*Opposite:* STEPPED MOULDING (top) and LARGE FLAT FACE FRAME
Both frames, made from obeche, have been water-gilded on black bole. The stepped moulding was gilded with high carat gold leaf. The white gold leaf frame was left to tarnish and features pastiglia (raised gesso work).
LEONARD VILLA FRAME-MAKERS and GILDERS and RIAN KANDUTH

*Above:* CARVED FRENCH
WALNUT FRAME
This frame was hand-
carved and incorporates
*rann d'el foliage* design on
either side of the face and
scrollwork and a stylized
flower design on the
horizontals.
Frame carved by
ROBERT RANDALL

*Left:* CASSETTA FRAME
This frame has been
water-gilded using white
gold leaf on blue bole and
the central section hand-
painted in black gouache.
The deckle-edged picture
was positioned on white
card leaving a narrow
border all around so that
the bevel of the stepped
window mount holds the
card and not the picture.
Frame by RIAN KANDUTH;
picture by NEIL PARK;
collection of ANDREW
JAKEMAN

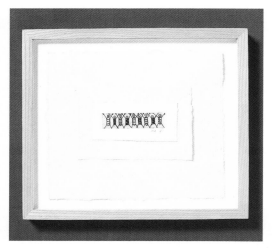

*Left:* HAND-BUILT
STEPPED FRAME
This frame has been
water-gilded using white
gold leaf on brown bole.
The narrow fillets are also
water-gilded. The window
mount is stepped as well
as embossed.
Frame by LEONARD VILLA
FRAMEMAKERS AND
GILDERS; picture by
ANDY KINGSBURY

*Above:* MEDIUM FLAT-
FACED FRAME
This ash frame has been
left in its natural state so
as not to overpower the
detailed deckle-edged
artwork. White-painted
wooden fillets were used
to raise the glass above
the artwork.
Frame by RIAN KANDUTH;
picture by DAMIEN SELL

*Left:* CARVED OAK
FRAME
This hand-carved frame
incorporates Grinling
Gibbons style foliage,
grapes and husks, with
acanthus leaves in the
corners. The wood has
been left untreated.
Frame carved by
ASHLEY SANDS

*Above:* LARGE HALF-
ROUND FRAME
This ash frame has been
stained dark oak and
incorporates white fillets.
The picture has been laid
on silk mountboard.
RIAN KANDUTH

# MATERIALS

THE MATERIALS LISTED BELOW ARE FAIRLY INEXPENSIVE AND THE MAJORITY CAN BE PURCHASED AT ART SHOPS, HARDWARE STORES AND BUILDER'S MERCHANTS. HOWEVER, GOLD LEAF IS EXPENSIVE. IT IS ADVISABLE TO PRACTISE WITH A CHEAPER TYPE OF LEAF, SUCH AS DUTCH METAL LEAF, WHICH COMES IN VARIOUS COLOURS. WHEN PROFICIENT IN HANDLING THE LEAF, GRADUATE TO REAL GOLD LEAF.

**Acrylic gesso** Used to provide a very smooth base to a frame. It can be sanded to porcelain smoothness.

**Acrylic varnish** Available in different sheens from high gloss to matt. Acrylic varnish has a much faster drying time than spirit-(alcohol-) based varnishes and is more pleasant to work with. Craquelure is a two-part varnish, available at most art shops, which produces a crackled effect.

**Backing tape** Applied to the back of the frame and hardboard to cover the pins and to prevent dust entering. The self-adhesive type is recommended.

**Barrier board** Available in various colours and pH values (pH7 is neutral, pH below 7 is acidic, pH above 7 is alkaline). For the protection of artwork it is advisable to use a neutral pH.

**Birch plywood** A construction material consisting of thin sheets of wood glued together. The woodgrains of adjacent sheets are arranged at right angles to each other, which makes the plywood exceptionally strong for its light weight. It has an unusual and pleasing pattern.

**Cloth** Useful for applying oil or oil paints, and for cleaning glass.

**Cork sanding block** This tool is useful when sanding flat surfaces, as it will help to avoid making dips in the surface.

**Danish oil** Applied to unprimed wood, this will slightly darken the wood and will result in a natural sheen.

**Epoxy resin** A very strong adhesive used in framing with metal, stone or glass.

**Etching spray** Used for creating patterns on glass; available at most good art shops.

**Fillet** A thin length of wood used to separate glass from artwork or when framing a canvas.

**Fine black marker pen** Used for marking glass when measuring and cutting.

**Gaffer tape** Exceptionally strong industrial tape, available from most hardware stores.

**Gelatine capsules** When melted in hot water, these capsules produce an adhering solution for use in *verre eglomisé*.

**Glass** Picture glass is usually 2 mm (⅛ in) thick and up to 1 m (1 yd) long. Larger pieces of glass are more dense, approximately 4–6 mm (¼ in) thick. Museum glass is extremely expensive, but for precious artwork it is recommended. Non-reflective glass has a cloudy etched look and can be quite distracting.

**Gold and silver leaf** Numerous sorts of leaf are available. Gold is very expensive; Dutch metal or silver leaf are cheaper alternatives. Leaf is available either loose or on transfer sheets.

**Gouache** A water-based paint, more opaque and economical than watercolour paints. Gouache is obtainable at all good art shops.

**Hardboard** Several types and thicknesses of hardboard are available. The most commonly used is 3 mm (⅛ in) thick.

**Lacquer** There are various types of lacquer available, water-based and spirit-(alcohol-) based. Acrylic varnish is used in woodstaining.

**Lime wax** This consists of clear wax with whiting which collects in the grain of the wood and results in a pale limed effect.

**Metal foils** Thin sheets of copper, brass and aluminium, available in art shops.

**Metal polish** A very fine abrasive cream. It may be used for any shellac-based project to give the frame's surface a glossy appearance.

**Methylated spirits** This solvent is used as a thinner for woodstain and to clean paintbrushes.

**Mount board** There is a wide range of mount card available, falling mainly into two categories, regular and conservation. Conservation mount card is acid-free.

**Nylon thread** Available from most haberdashery (notions) and fishing stores.

**Oil size for gilding** Available at any good art shop, and used in oil gilding as a mordant. It is available with different drying times: the longer the drying time, the shinier the gold leaf.

**Paints** Gouache is very opaque and economical and gives a professional finish. Acrylic paints are more translucent than gouache, and less expensive. Oil paints can also be used as a finish.

**Pigments** These are the purest form of paint and are extremely strong.

**Pumice powder** A powder abrasive used in this book for distressing *verre eglomisé*. Different grades are available.

**Rotring pen** Used for fine penwork.

**Sandpaper** Available in different grades from fine to coarse. Wet and dry sandpaper is economical as it is reusable.

**Self-adhesive lead** Available in different widths and sold in most hardware shops.

**Shellac** Also known as special pale polish and used on wood.

**Silk screen cleaner** Available at specialist art shops.

**Spatula** A small spatula is extremely useful for filling in mitres on the frame and for mixing epoxy resin.

**Spray lacquer** Available in black and clear at car shops. It is vital that lacquer is used carefully in a well-ventilated area. Always wear a safety mask.

**Stencil card** (Card stock) Thin card treated to make it strong and reusable.

**Tape** There are various self-adhesive tapes available for taping up the back of a frame. Double-sided tape may be used with small frames to secure fillets.

**Teak oil** A darkish oil for use on unprimed wood. It results in a natural warm sheen.

**Tracing paper** Used to copy designs and transfer them on to a frame.

**Wax** Clear wax is used to coat and enrich different types of wood.

**White chinagraph pencil** Used to mark metal, plastics, dark fabrics or glass temporarily.

**White spirit** This solvent is used for oil size, and for cleaning brushes when using oil-based products.

**Wire (steel) wool** Used for sanding and scoring surfaces, and for applying liming wax.

**Wood glue** PVA (white) wood glue is used for securing all wood.

**Wood oil** Danish and teak oil are applied to unprimed wood. Linseed oil may also be used, but it is not as dark as Danish or teak oil. All oils absorb into the wood, and some take longer than others to dry; follow the manufacturer's instructions.

**Woodfiller** Used to fill in gaps on mitred corners and after punching nails into wood. Various types of filler are available.

**Woodstain** Available in an abundance of colours and types, from crystals to solutions. Woodstain can be bought from art shops and hardware stores.

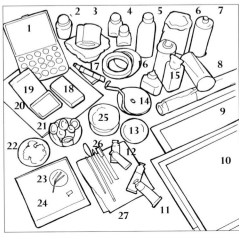

KEY

| | |
|---|---|
| **1** Pigments | **15** Glue and lacquer |
| **2** Metal finish | **16** Masking tape and |
| **3** Cotton and wire wool | backing tape |
| **4** Craquelure varnish | **17** Epoxy resin |
| **5** Methylated spirits | **18** Cork sanding block |
| **6** Interior filler | **19** Gold leaf |
| **7** Etching spray | **20** Sandpaper |
| **8** Metal foils | **21** Woodstains |
| **9** Hardboard/barrier | **22** Clear wax |
| board | **23** Sewing needles |
| **10** Mount board | **24** Velvet |
| **11** Oil paints | **25** Lime wax |
| **12** Gouache/watercolour | **26** Rotring pen/ |
| **13** White spirit | chinagraph/spatulas |
| **14** Self-adhesive lead | **27** Cloth |

# EQUIPMENT

SOME OF THE EQUIPMENT LISTED BELOW IS BASIC FRAME-MAKING EQUIPMENT, WHICH YOU WILL USE AGAIN AND AGAIN. OTHER ITEMS, FOR EXAMPLE THE GILDING TOOLS, ARE ONLY REQUIRED FOR PARTICULAR PROJECTS. SPECIALIST TOOLS, SUCH AS A FRAMER'S PIN GUN, ARE AVAILABLE FROM FRAMING SUPPLIERS.

**Blade** Required for mount cutting to release the cut corners of the window mount to avoid tearing.

**Bradawl** Used for making initial holes in hardboard or wood.

**Burnishing tool** Used to polish raised areas of a metal finish.

**Clamps** These come in all shapes and sizes and have various uses. A mitre clamp is a metal fixture, usually bolted to a work bench, in which moulding lengths are inserted and cut at a 45-degree angle.

**Craft knife** This has multiple uses in picture framing. There are several varieties so choose one that feels comfortable.

**Cutting mat** Essential for cutting on, as it protects the underlying surface.

**Drill and drill bits** Both electric and hand drills are suitable.

**D-rings** There is a vast range of hinges available. D-rings are available single or double (for larger frames). Attach them to the hardboard with butterflies (rivet-like fixings), or screw directly into the back of the frame.

**Framer's pin gun** This tool is for fitting up picture frames. It inserts flat pins into the moulding, which hold the hardboard securely in place.

**Gilder's cushion** Gold leaf is laid on top of this before being cut.

**Gilder's knife** A special knife used for cutting gold leaf.

**Gilder's tip** Used for picking up gold leaf and applying it to the surface.

**Glass cutter** Diamond-headed and tungsten types for heavy-duty glass cutting can be quite expensive. There are cheaper alternatives for domestic use.

**Hacksaw** Used in a mitre clamp to cut wooden or manufactured mouldings. There are various types of saw blade, including blades for cutting metal mouldings.

**Hand-held underpinner tool** This has many uses. When joining the frame it acts as a hand-held underpinner, pushing "V" pins into the joined mitre cuts and holding the frame together. It is also capable of securing the hardboard to the frame.

**Heatgun** An electrical appliance used for burning in patterns in wooden mouldings.

**Mitre box** A box for cutting moulding lengths at a 45-degree angle.

**Mitre clamp** A metal fixture, usually bolted to a bench, into which mouldings are inserted and cut at a 45-degree angle.

**Mount cutter** A tool for cutting a bevelled window out of mount board. Buy hand-held ones at good art shops.

**Paintbrushes** Use flat-face oil and sable brushes, approximately 1 cm (½ in) and 2.5 cm (1 in) wide for detailing and pointing. Use stencil brushes for stencilling.

**Panel pins (Brads)** Thin pins used for joining frames and tacking hardboard to a frame in the final assembly stage; an alternative to the hand-held underpinner tool.

**Safety gloves** Use latex gloves for painting, and protective gloves for metal foils and when cutting glass.

**Safety mask** Use with any sprays to avoid inhalation.

**Straight edge rule** Akin to a ruler, this tool is more industrial.

**Tack hammer** A lightweight hammer used for joining frames.

**Tape measure** Used for measuring artwork, mounts and moulding.

**Tenon saw** A 30 cm (12 in) wide, flat saw used with a mitre box to cut wooden or manufactured mouldings.

**T–square** A measuring tool used to give a true square or rectangle. Used when measuring mounts and cutting glass.

**"V" pins** Used with the hand-held underpinner tool to underpin the frame.

**Wire cutters** Used to cut metal foil and hanging wire.

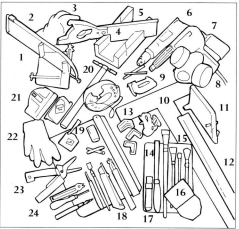

KEY
1 Mitre clamp
2 Hacksaw
3 Safety gloves
4 Tenon saw
5 Mitre box
6 Drill and bits
7 Heatgun
8 Safety mask
9 G-clamp
10 T-square
11 Framer's pin gun
12 Straight edge rule
13 Clamp
14 Gilder's cushion and knife
15 Paintbrushes
16 Gilder's tip
17 Stencil brush
18 Ruler/hand-held underpinner tool/craft knife/glass cutter/scalpel/"V"-pins
19 Tape measure/eraser/blade/cutting mat
20 Tack hammer
21 Mount cutter
22 Latex gloves
23 Wire cutters
24 Plastic burnishing tool/bradawl/burnishing tool

# BASIC TECHNIQUES

THE TECHNIQUES USED THROUGHOUT THIS BOOK ARE NOT DIFFICULT TO LEARN, AND CAN BE EASILY MASTERED AFTER A LITTLE PRACTICE. IT IS VERY IMPORTANT TO TAKE PRECISE MEASUREMENTS AND IT IS OFTEN WORTHWHILE DOUBLE-CHECKING YOUR MEASUREMENTS BEFORE YOU CUT ANYTHING. ONCE YOU HAVE MADE YOUR FRAME, CHOOSE A SUITABLE PLACE TO HANG IT AND THE BEST FIXINGS TO USE FOR EACH KIND OF FRAME.

## MEASURING A PICTURE FOR A MOUNT

The primary purpose of a mount is to separate the artwork from the glass. Since paper fibres tend to expand and contract with temperature and humidity changes, which results in buckling or waving of the artwork, the mount allows room for movement inside the frame. The wide range of mount boards available fall mainly into two categories, regular and conservation. Regular boards gradually become acidic over the years and can damage your artwork. Conservation boards, however, are acid-free and will not damage artwork. Where a mount is not used, it is recommended that fillets are used to prevent the glass from touching the artwork.

The mount must always be larger than the artwork. It is customary to allow a larger margin at the bottom of the mount than at the top or the sides to correct an optical illusion which occurs when the picture is hung on the wall. If all the margins were the same width, the bottom one would appear smaller than the others.

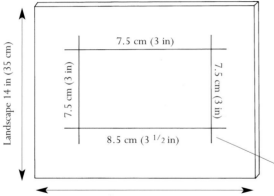

Landscape 14 in (35 cm)

7.5 cm (3 in)

7.5 cm (3 in)

7.5 cm (3 in)

8.5 cm (3 1/2 in)

Landscape 14 in (35 cm)

Pencil mark measurements and crossovers

1 Measure the picture horizontally, and add on 7.5 cm (3 in) to both sides. This will give you the landscape measurement.

2 Measure the picture vertically, adding on 7.5 cm (3 in) at the top and 8.5 cm (3½ in) at the bottom. This will give you the portrait measurement (see diagram for guide).

3 Following the measurements, cut the mount board to size. Mark inner measurements on to the mount board using the tape measure. Join up the measurements with a ruler and pencil to mark the pencilled window.

4 Line up the straight edge against the edge of the mount, push the mount cutter blade into the board and move the mount cutter steadily along the marked line to cut out the window. Go over the pencil mark crossovers slightly, to avoid cross-cuts on the face of the mount.

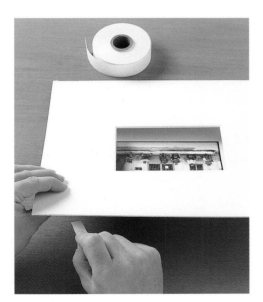

5 Once you have cut out the window, carefully place a blade into each corner and trim the cut edge to release the centre freely. This will avoid any tearing of the corners. Erase the pencil marks.

6 Place the window mount face up on the picture below it, and line them up. Attach the picture to the mount using acid-free hinging tape on the top edges of the artwork.

## SINGLE WINDOW MOUNT

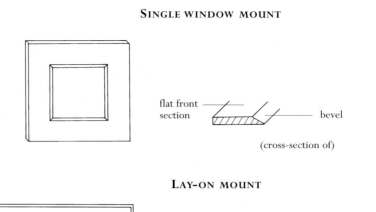

flat front section — bevel

(cross-section of)

## LAY-ON MOUNT

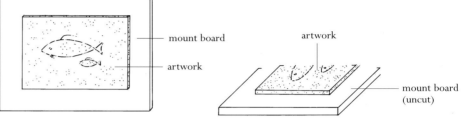

mount board

artwork

artwork

mount board (uncut)

## BOOK MOUNT

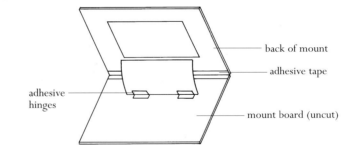

back of mount

adhesive tape

adhesive hinges

mount board (uncut)

## FLOAT MOUNT

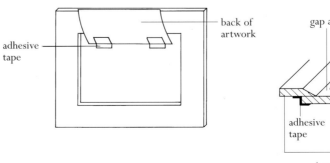

back of artwork

adhesive tape

gap all around artwork

artwork

front mount

adhesive tape

mount board (uncut)

back section

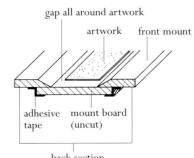

## CUTTING AND JOINING A FRAME

There are several ways of cutting a section of moulding, using either a mitre clamp or a wooden mitre box. When joining the frame, a few basic tools are required: a vice, a frame clamp, a hand-held underpinner tool and a framer's pin gun.

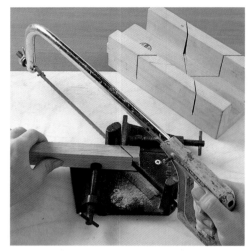

1 Measure the artwork for the mount to give you the inside rebate measurement for the frame. Start by cutting the moulding length at a 45-degree angle, as shown. The edge of the moulding with the rebate should be the furthest from you.

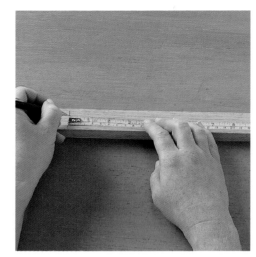

2 Measure along the inside rebate of the moulding and mark the first cut on the face of the moulding.

3 Insert the moulding into the mitre clamp or box and cut with a saw at a 45-degree angle.

4 Place the moulding in the mitre clamp or box. To make the next section of the frame, cut away the triangle "offcut" as in step 1 with the same 45-degree angle. Do this before you measure the second cut.

5 Measure and mark the second cut on the moulding. Repeat the above steps until all four lengths are cut. To check that they are the correct length, hold them together and place your fingertips on the edges of the cuts. They should feel flush.

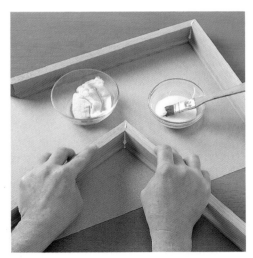

6 Using PVA (white) wood glue, stick two sections of the moulding together to make a right angle. Repeat with the other sections, then join them all together to make the frame.

7 Place the frame clamp round the frame to hold the glued pieces together. Wipe away excess PVA glue with a damp cloth. Be sure to clean off excess glue otherwise colourwash or woodstain will not take to the wood.

8 Once the frame is secured in the frame clamp, turn the frame face down, then place underpins into the corners of the back of the frame using a hand-held underpinner tool. Or, place the right-angled corners of the frame in a vice, and hammer panel pins (brads) into the corner edges of the moulding using a tack hammer. Once all four corners have been pinned, leave overnight to dry.

9 Turn the frame right side up and fill in the mitred corners with woodfiller. Wipe away excess woodfiller with a damp cloth.

10 Once the woodfiller has set (this will vary depending on the type of filler you use, but usually it will be an hour or so), use a cork sanding block and coarse-grade sandpaper to sand all over the frame and the rebate. Repeat with finer-grade sandpaper.

## GLASS CUTTING

There are various types and thicknesses of picture glass available. Picture glass is usually thinner than window glass and without flaws. Glass is required on any artwork needing protection from atmospheric pollution and ultraviolet rays, which in time will cause a picture to fade. The most commonly used glass is 2 mm (⅛ in) clear glass. For more precious artwork museum glass is used; although extremely expensive, it is undoubtedly the best protection for artwork and it is almost invisible. Non-reflective glass has a cloudy etched appearance. For reasons of safety, 2 mm (⅛ in) glass is used only up to a certain size, approximately 1 m (1 yd). For areas larger than this, over-sized heavy-duty 4–6 mm (¼ in) glass should be used or, alternatively, perspex may be substituted.

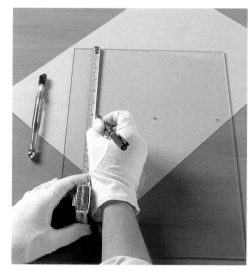

2 Reduce this measurement by 3 mm (⅛ in), then mark the measurement on the glass using a fine black marker.

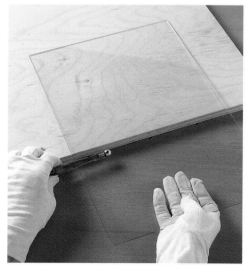

4 Holding the glass over a board so that the score line is on the edge, gently tap the glass below the score mark, using the round end of the cutter.

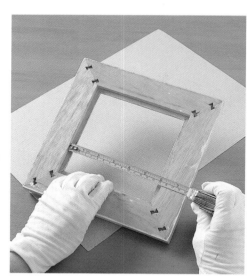

1 On the reverse side of the frame, measure the horizontal inside from rebate to rebate. Wear protective cotton gloves when you are handling glass.

3 Place a T-square on the glass and line up the glass cutter so that it is on top of the marks. Holding both the glass cutter and T-square, firmly but gently score the glass in one long smooth stroke with the glass cutter. Do not cut over the same cut, as this will make the glass shatter and splinter.

5 Place a pencil directly beneath the cut. Using both hands placed on either side of the pencil and score mark, gently but firmly press the glass down. The glass will break cleanly along the score line.

## ASSEMBLING A FRAME

"Fitting up" is the process of fixing the artwork into the frame itself. It is advisable to follow the simple steps below and assemble the sections in the correct order.

**6** Repeat steps 1–5 for the vertical measurement.

**7** When the glass is cut, gently insert it in the rebate at the back of the frame.

**1** Measure the artwork then measure and cut the mount. Adhere the artwork by hinging it to the back of the mount board as in this single window mount. Cut out the barrier board and hardboard and place these beneath the mounted board. Measure the inside rebate, vertical and horizontal. Mark and cut the glass to the correct size.

**2** Place the glass on a soft white background (to see dust and dirt), and clean with a soft cloth and methylated spirits. Place the artwork, barrier board and hard board below the clean glass.

**3** Place the frame over the glass, artwork, barrier board and hardboard. Hold up the frame and layers vertically and check for dust.

**4** Remove the hardboard from the back of the frame, keeping the other layers together. Make two level holes in the hardboard with a bradawl, not too close to the centre or edge. Place D-rings on top of the holes and insert a butterfly rivet through the hole of the D-ring and the hole in the hardboard.

▶

**5** Turn the hardboard over (reverse or non-wall side showing), place a nail punch (or a long nail) between the "wings" of the butterfly and hammer on the nail punch. This will open the butterfly. Once opened, hammer the butterfly fully open and flat.

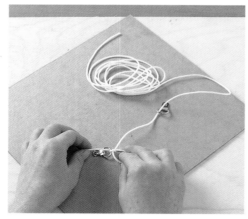

**6** Turn the hardboard over, (front or wall side showing) and insert the picture cord through the D-rings, wrapping it around each D-ring twice.

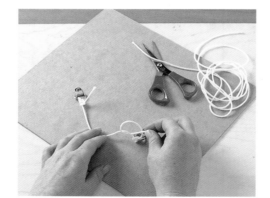

**7** Tie the picture cord using overhand knots, approximately four knots on each side. If the picture is over 60 cm (2 ft) in length or height, it is advisable to use a cow hitch knot in the first D-ring. This type of knot will double up the picture cord, enabling it to take more weight. Use five or six overhand knots in the second D-ring.

**8** Turn the frame over and put the hardboard in place over the back of the frame. Hold down the frame at the corners with one hand and use the pin gun with the other hand. This safeguards the mitred corners from popping open. Secure the frame layers by using the framer's pin gun to insert flat pins into the frame, as shown. An alternative way of pinning in the hardboard is by using panel pins (brads) and a tack hammer; place the pins flat on the hard-board and hammer them part of the way into the moulding as for the gun pins.

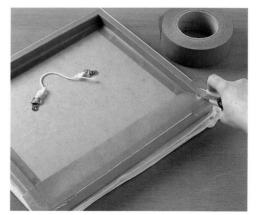

**9** Place backing tape on the back of the frame, not too close to the edge of the frame, approximately ⅛ in (3 mm) away, otherwise the tape may be visible once the picture is hanging on the wall. Cut the tape with a craft knife down the outer edge of the frame, then fold the tape down.

### KNOTS

Cow hitch knot

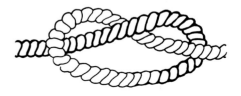

Overhand knot

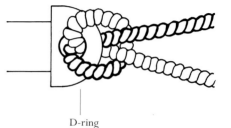

D-ring

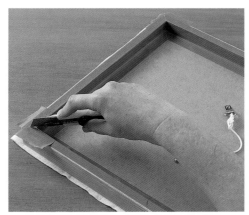

**10** Using the craft knife, cut neat mitres in the backing tape on all four corners. Cut the tape where it covers both the hardboard and the moulding.

**11** Remove the excess tape from both sides of each mitred corner.

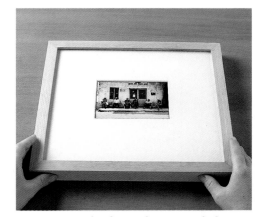

**12** Turn the frame face up and clean the glass with methylated spirits and a soft cloth. Polish up the frame using a separate cloth.

## ORDER OF FITTING UP FOR WINDOW MOUNTS

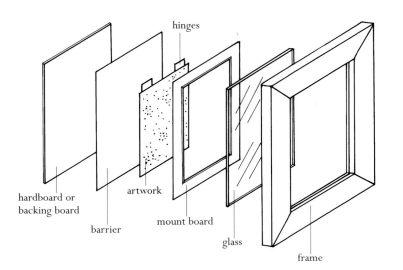

hinges

hardboard or backing board

barrier

artwork

mount board

glass

frame

## ORDER OF FITTING UP FOR LAY-ON OR DIMENSIONAL OBJECTS

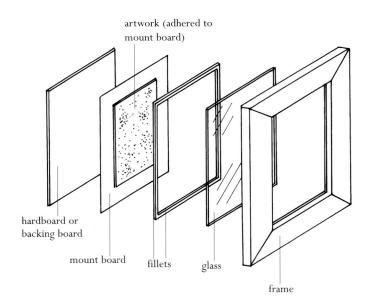

artwork (adhered to mount board)

hardboard or backing board

mount board

fillets

glass

frame

## MOULDINGS

Moulding is the shaped wood which will ultimately be composed into the frame itself. Mouldings are referred to by their profile, ie the cross-section or end-view. Mouldings are usually sold in 1.8 m or 2.4 m (6 ft or 8 ft) lengths, from a builders' merchant, timber yard, specialist art shop or framer.

There are two basic types of moulding, picture frame moulding and builders' moulding. The principal contrast between the two is that picture frame moulding includes a fitted rebate, a step that allows the artwork, mount, glass and hardboard to fit uniformly into place without collapsing through the frame. Builders' moulding is fundamentally intended for trimming internal structures such as door frames, windows and skirting boards, and consequently does not incorporate a fitted rebate. To convert builders' moulding it is necessary to create a recess by sticking a narrow strip of wood such as a fillet underneath the moulding.

Manufactured moulding is pre-decorated and finished. There is an impressive array of manufactured mouldings available, from reproduction, antiqued, metal and highly decorated to plain, simple styles.

Natural wood mouldings leave the embellishment in the hands of the framer. Ash and oak have a pleasing grain, and lime-waxing and woodstaining these types of wood bring out the best of the natural grain. Obeche and ramin are woods that are suitable for more opaque or solid decoration. One factor to take into consideration is whether the wood is a softwood or a hardwood. For example, ash and oak are very hard and take some perseverance to cut, whereas obeche, pine and ramin are fairly easy to cut.

## MANUFACTURED MOULDINGS

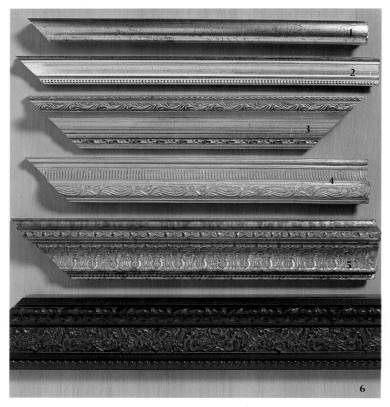

**1** Medium plain shaped moulding
**2** Medium shaped moulding, with beading on the rebate edge
**3** Large shaped moulding, with gold and silver finish
**4** Large reverse moulding, with gold finish
**5** Large foliage and waterleaf moulding, with gold finish
**6** Large foliage moulding, with lacquer finish

PARTS OF A MOULDING

TYPES OF MOULDINGS

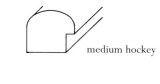

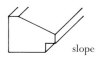

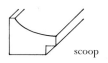

## NATURAL WOOD MOULDINGS

## NATURAL WOOD MOULDINGS

**1** Small flat face – pine
**2** Medium hockey/cushion – ash
**3** Medium flat face – oak
**4** Small swept – obeche
**5** Large swept – maple veneer
**6** Large flat-face angled bevel – ramin
**7** Large reverse moulding – ramin
**8 & 9** Large plain cassetta – obeche

**1** Reverse moulding – oak
**2** Cassetta – obeche
**3** Cassetta – ramin
**4** Swept obeche MDF, compressed decoration
**5** Large shaped ramin MDF, compressed decoration
**6** Large wavy – pine
**7** Large swept ramin MDF, compressed decoration

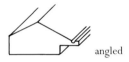

swept

angled

cut back angled

small cushion

rounded

reversed

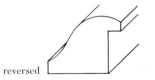

two different
types of cassetta

## FIXINGS

When hanging any artwork, it is vital to consider the weight and size of the frame. It is very easy to underestimate just how heavy a frame is and therefore the type of fixings needed to hold it in place.

You can use wire or cord for hanging more or less any weight of frame. Single or double D-rings are sufficiently strong fixings for light to mediumweight frames, but you should use strap hangers for heavy or large frames.

Single and double D-rings can be inserted either into the hardboard using rivets or butterflies, or screwed directly into the back section of the frame. The wire or cord is threaded through the first fixing, using a cow hitch knot to secure, and then through the second fixing and secured using five or six overhand knots. Strap hangers are screwed on to the back section of the frame and wire or cord can be attached in the same way. However, if the frame is particularly heavy, it is recommended to hang the picture from the loops of the strap hanger on to screws inserted directly into the wall (rather than using picture wire or cord).

Anti-theft devices (ATDs) and mirror plates work in much the same way as strap hangers. The straight section is screwed into the back of the frame, and the curved section is screwed to the wall.

Spring clips can be used instead of pins to secure artwork in a frame. Their advantage is that they can easily be removed if you want to replace the artwork. The flat edge of the clip is screwed into the back of the moulding and the curled edge lies on top of the hardboard, securing the artwork within.

KEY

1 Picture wire
2 Mirror plates
3 Anti-theft devices
4 Screws
5 Rivets or butterflies
6 Strap hangers
7 Spring clips
8 Picture cord
9 Double D-rings
10 Single D-rings

## PICTURE HANGING

There are a few considerations to bear in mind when you are deciding where to hang a picture. Avoid placing artworks where fluctuating temperatures and humidity changes may be experienced, for example near a heat source or on an outside wall. Condensation encourages mould and may also cause the paper to buckle. It is also inadvisable to hang a painting of any kind in strong light or direct sunlight because of heat, dust and exposure to ultra-violet light. Ultra-violet rays damage artworks irrevocably and colours will fade in time if exposed to high levels of light. Paper tends to absorb high-energy photons from light, which in turn causes a chemical reaction in the paper, ultimately breaking it down and causing it to become brittle.

Never underestimate the weight of a frame. If it is heavy, it is best to insert screws into the wall and hang it directly from strap hangers screwed into the frame. Do not use cord or wire to hang heavy frames as these may give way under the weight.

*Above: A successful frame will enhance the work it frames without distracting from the image. In a living room pictures may need to be hung at a slightly lower level than eye level as you will most often be sitting down when looking at the picture.*

*Left: Pictures are an integral part of the decoration of your rooms. They should blend in with the interior and you should take into account the light and colour scheme of the furniture and walls when you decide where to hang a picture. Pictures grouped together can look very effective.*

*Right: The image and frame enhance the atmosphere of a muted colour scheme, faded walls and washed floorboards.*

# DECORATIVE WINDOW MOUNT

THERE IS AN ABUNDANCE OF DECORATIVE PAPERS AVAILABLE, ANY OF WHICH MAY BE CUT INTO STRIPS OR ABSTRACT GEOMETRIC SHAPES AND USED TO TRANSFORM A SIMPLE PRE-CUT MOUNT INTO SOMETHING SPECIAL. ALTERNATIVELY, YOU COULD COVER THE ENTIRE WINDOW MOUNT IN A SINGLE DECORATIVE PAPER, FOLLOWING THE SAME TECHNIQUE FOR CUTTING AND GLUING THAT IS USED IN THE Velvet-covered Mount PROJECT.

**1** On the face of the pre-cut window mount, mark out light lines with a pencil and ruler or straight edge, setting out where the decorative border is to be placed.

**2** Place the decorative paper on a cutting mat to protect the surface and, using a craft knife and ruler, measure and cut the paper into appropriate-sized strips.

**3** Apply spray mount or PVA (white) glue on the reverse of the cut strips. Stick the strips to the markings on the face of the mount. Press down gently to secure.

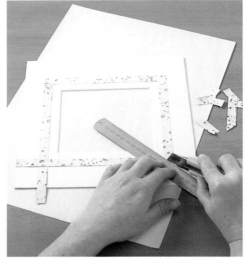

**4** Using a ruler and craft knife, carefully cut mitres on all four corners of the decorative strips. Remove excess paper once mitres have been cut.

MATERIALS AND EQUIPMENT YOU WILL NEED

PRE-CUT MOUNT • 2B (#2) SOFT PENCIL • RULER OR STRAIGHT EDGE • DECORATIVE PAPER • CUTTING MAT •
CRAFT KNIFE • SPRAY MOUNT OR PVA (WHITE) GLUE

# STEPPED WINDOW MOUNT

THIS DESIGN IS SIMILAR TO A NORMAL SINGLE WINDOW MOUNT BUT WITH THE ADDITION OF A SECOND MOUNT, FEATURING A SLIGHTLY LARGER WINDOW OPENING, STUCK ON TOP. THIS RESULTS IN AN INTERESTING STEPPED LOOK, AND PRODUCES A STUNNING EFFECT WHEN MADE IN DIFFERENT-COLOURED MOUNT BOARD. EXPERIMENT WITH VARIOUS COLOUR COMBINATIONS TO MAKE THE MOST ORDINARY PICTURE LOOK GOOD. THE "STEP" MAY BE INCREASED OR DECREASED.

1 Measure the picture vertically and horizontally (see Basic Techniques). Following the measurements, cut two pieces of mount board the same size. The size of the mount is a matter of personal preference.

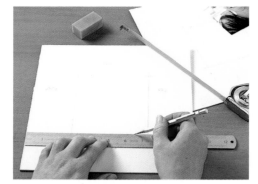

2 Mark the measurements of the picture on one piece of board. Then, on the other piece, mark the original measurements reducing the mount size by 1 cm (½ in). For example, if the original measurements are 7.5 cm (3 in) at the sides and top, and 8.5 cm (3½ in) at the bottom, the measurements on the other piece of board would be 6.5 cm (2½ in) for the sides and top, and 7.5 cm (3 in) at the bottom.

4 Erase the pencil marks and apply PVA (white) glue on to the back of the reduced measurement mount. Place this on to the face of the original measurement mount. Press down to ensure good adhesion.

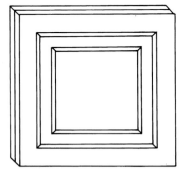

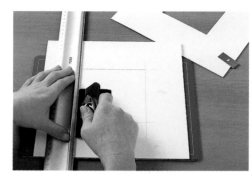

3 Cut out the windows on each board using a mount cutter and blade.

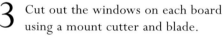

This (flat) area may be increased or decreased

MATERIALS AND EQUIPMENT YOU WILL NEED

TAPE MEASURE • MOUNT CUTTER • CUTTING MAT • 2 PIECES OF MOUNT BOARD • 2B (#2) PENCIL • STRAIGHT EDGE • T-SQUARE • BLADE • ERASER • PVA (WHITE) GLUE AND BRUSH

# VELVET-COVERED MOUNT

FABRIC-COVERED MOUNTS ADD AN IMMENSE AMOUNT OF RICHNESS AND DEPTH TO AN OBJECT OR A PICTURE, ESPECIALLY IF YOU USE A LUXURY FABRIC SUCH AS SILK, BROCADE OR VELVET. IN THE PAST, PERSIAN AND INDIAN TEXTILES WERE OFTEN FRAMED BY A FABRIC-COVERED MOUNT. BE CAREFUL IF YOU ARE USING A THIN FABRIC SUCH AS SILK AS THE GLUE MAY SEEP THROUGH THE FABRIC, SO ONLY GLUE THE OVERLAPS ON THE REVERSE.

1 Place the pre-cut mount face down on to the velvet on a cutting mat. Leaving 2.5 cm (1 in) of fabric all around for overlaps, cut out the velvet with a craft knife.

2 Cut off the corners of the fabric to make folding over easier. Apply a thin, even coat of fabric glue to the face of the mount.

3 Place the fabric evenly on top of the mount, press down and rub gently with a cloth, or use a lino-(linoleum-) cut roller to ensure good adhesion. ▶

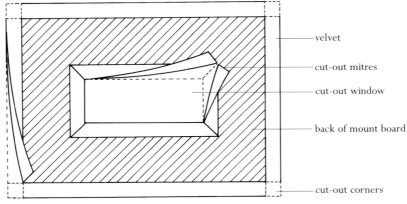

- velvet
- cut-out mitres
- cut-out window
- back of mount board
- cut-out corners

## MATERIALS AND EQUIPMENT YOU WILL NEED

PRE-CUT MOUNT • VELVET • CUTTING MAT • CRAFT KNIFE • RULER • FABRIC GLUE AND BRUSH • SOFT CLOTH OR LINO-(LINOLEUM-) CUT ROLLER

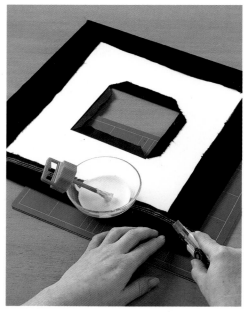

4 Turn over the covered mount so that the velvet fabric is face down. Cut a small square in the fabric in the window, leaving an extra amount of fabric for the overlaps.

5 Cut mitres in the overlap fabric in the window. Apply fabric glue on the mount where the overlaps will lie, then fold over the overlap fabric and press down firmly.

6 Fold down the overlaps on the side edges of the mount. At the corners, hold the velvet firmly and cut a mitre with a craft knife, then apply fabric glue and press the fabric down. Allow to dry.

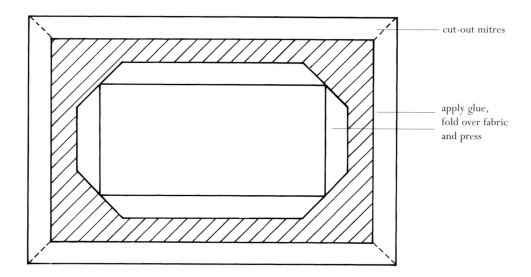

cut-out mitres

apply glue, fold over fabric and press

# MULTIPLE WINDOW MOUNT

SOMETIMES MORE THAN ONE WINDOW MOUNT IS REQUIRED, PERHAPS FOR A GROUP OF PHOTOGRAPHS OR ARTWORKS, OR TO MAKE A TRIPTYCH. CUTTING A MULTIPLE WINDOW MOUNT IS NOT AN EASY TASK TO MASTER AT FIRST; GREAT CARE AND CONCENTRATION IS NEEDED WHEN MEASURING AND MARKING THE ARTWORK, AND IT IS WELL WORTH DOUBLE-CHECKING YOUR MEASUREMENTS BEFORE YOU MAKE ANY CUTS.

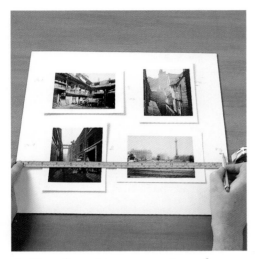

1 Place four pictures on a piece of mount board. Mark the horizontal measurements of the top two and bottom two pictures in pencil, just touching the pictures on all sides.

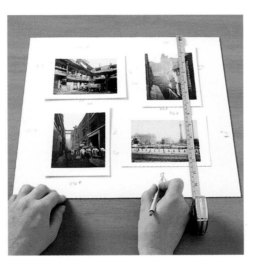

2 Next mark the vertical measurements of the top and bottom pictures in pencil, again just touching the pictures on all sides.

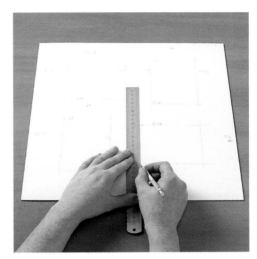

3 Once measurements have been marked, join them up using a pencil and a ruler. Be sure to make crossovers, so when cutting the mount you will know where to stop. ▶

MATERIALS AND EQUIPMENT YOU WILL NEED

MOUNT BOARD • 2B (#2) PENCIL • TAPE MEASURE • RULER • T-SQUARE • MOUNT CUTTER • CUTTING MAT • BLADE • ERASER • ACID-FREE HINGING TAPE

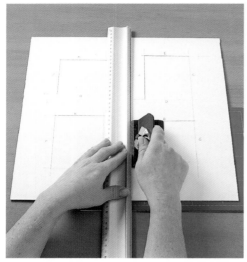

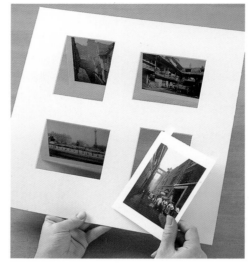

**4** Cut out the four windows, following the diagram below for the order of cutting. Move the mount board as you work, so you are cutting vertically. Erase the pencil marks.

**5** When all the windows have been cut, hinge the pictures as in a single mount (see Basic Techniques).

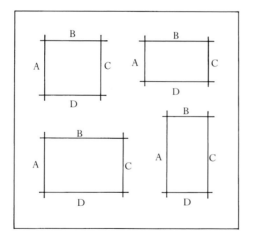

Back of
mount with
pencil marks

Cut in order of:
all A first
all B second
all C third
all D fourth

# LIME-WAXED FRAME

LIMING WAX IS A MIXTURE OF WHITE PIGMENT BLENDED WITH CLEAR WAX AND IS USUALLY APPLIED TO WOOD WITH AN ATTRACTIVE GRAIN, SUCH AS OAK OR ASH. THE WHITE PIGMENT SITS IN THE RELIEF GRAIN OF THE WOOD, WHILE THE RAISED GRAIN REMAINS BEAUTIFULLY TRANSLUCENT. THIS TRADITIONAL TECHNIQUE IS ONCE AGAIN FASHIONABLE FOR KITCHEN DOORS AND FURNITURE, AND IT WORKS EQUALLY WELL ON A PICTURE FRAME THAT WILL LOOK RIGHT IN MANY SITUATIONS.

1 Sand the frame all over initially with coarse-grade then with fine-grade sandpaper for a smooth surface.

2 Using wire (steel) wool, pick up some liming wax from the tin and apply it to the frame in long even strokes, continuing all round the frame. Work the wax into the woodgrain as you go.

3 Apply a second coat of liming wax to achieve a deeper effect.

4 When you have covered the frame completely, gently polish the liming wax with a cloth. Do not use too much pressure as this will wipe off the previously applied wax.

## MATERIALS AND EQUIPMENT YOU WILL NEED

JOINED AND SANDED WOODEN FRAME • COARSE- AND FINE-GRADE SANDPAPER • WIRE (STEEL) WOOL • LIMING WAX • CLOTH

# COLOURWASHED FRAME

COLOURWASHING INVOLVES USING ACRYLIC, EMULSION (LATEX) OR GOUACHE PAINTS. DEPENDING ON THE DENSITY OF THE SOLUTION, THE WASH CAN BE EITHER TRANSLUCENT OR OPAQUE. THE MORE TRANSLUCENT THE WASH, THE MORE OF THE WOODGRAIN WILL BE APPARENT. COLOURWASHING IS EASILY REVERSIBLE BY SANDING OFF THE COLOUR, AS IT DOES NOT PENETRATE AS DEEPLY INTO THE WOOD AS WOODSTAIN.

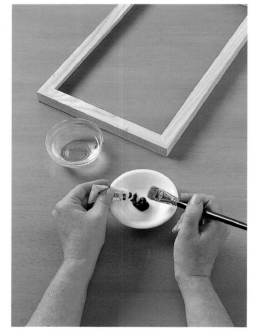

1 Sand the frame. Place a walnut size amount of gouache into a bowl, add a small amount of water initially and blend in thoroughly. The more water now added, the more translucent the wash will be; the less water added, the more opaque the wash will be. Test the strength of the wash on the back of the frame. Dip the paintbrush into the diluted water then wipe the paintbrush on the side of the bowl, removing excess paint.

2 Apply the wash to one section of the face of the frame in one smooth even stroke, from mitre join to mitre join. Then paint the side section of the frame. Continue all around the frame. Leave to dry for at least 15 minutes. The more coats of wash, the more opaque the wood will appear. Two coats are recommended. Clean the brush thoroughly with water.

3 When the wash is completely dry, lightly sand the frame with fine-grade sandpaper. This will slightly distress the wash and give a smooth finish.

4 For a wax finish, cover your index finger with a cloth, dip it in wax and work it in on a small piece of hardboard (this will soften the wax and make it easier to use). With one long, smooth stroke lightly apply the wax to the frame; do not rub it in as it may remove the wash. Continue all around the frame. Once finished, lightly rub in the wax from where you began. Two or three coats of wax may be applied for the required finish.

MATERIALS AND EQUIPMENT YOU WILL NEED
SPECTRUM VIOLET GOUACHE PAINT • GLASS BOWL • 2.5 CM (1 IN) FLAT SABLE PAINTBRUSH • JOINED AND SANDED ASH OR OAK FRAME •
FINE-GRADE SANDPAPER • CLOTH • CLEAR WAX • HARDBOARD OFFCUT (SCRAP)

# WOODSTAINED FRAME

THERE IS A WIDE VARIETY OF DIFFERENT WOODSTAINS ON THE MARKET NOWADAYS. THE DIFFERENCE BETWEEN A STAIN AND A WASH IS THAT THE STAIN WILL ACTUALLY PENETRATE THE WOOD SIGNIFICANTLY DEEPER THAN A WASH, AND WILL ALWAYS LET THE GRAIN OF THE WOOD SHOW THROUGH. BRUSHES SHOULD BE CLEANED THOROUGHLY WITH METHYLATED SPIRITS WHEN USING A SPIRIT-BASED STAIN, OR WATER WHEN USING A WATER-BASED STAIN.

1 Sand the frame for a smooth finish. For an opaque result, use pure undiluted woodstain. For a more translucent finish, dilute the woodstain with methylated spirits (turpentine) or appropriate solvent. Decant the mixture into a glass bowl. Wear latex gloves when working with woodstain.

2 Dip the paintbrush into the solution, wiping the excess on the side of the bowl. Apply the stain to the face of the frame, from mitre to mitre, in one long, smooth, even stroke. Continue on to the side edge and then all around the frame. Leave to dry for 10–15 minutes.

4 When the woodstain is dry to the touch, apply a coat of acrylic varnish. Leave to dry before applying one or two more coats as required.

3 Two or three coats of woodstain may be required to achieve a deeper colour.

## MATERIALS AND EQUIPMENT YOU WILL NEED

SANDPAPER • FRAME • SPIRIT (ALCOHOL-BASED) WOODSTAIN • METHYLATED SPIRITS • GLASS BOWL • LATEX GLOVES • 2.5 CM (1 IN) FLAT SABLE PAINTBRUSH • ACRYLIC VARNISH

# CRAQUELURE FRAME

MAKING A CRAQUELURE FRAME INVOLVES USING A TWO PART VARNISH CALLED CRAQUELURE. ONE IS SLOW DRYING, WHILE THE OTHER IS FAST DRYING. THE VARNISH SHRINKS SLIGHTLY AS IT DRIES, SO AS THE SLOW-DRYING LOWER LAYER CONTRACTS IT CAUSES CRACKING IN THE DRY LAYER OF VARNISH ABOVE. IT IS ADVISABLE TO EXPERIMENT WITH THIS TECHNIQUE AS TIMING AND ATMOSPHERIC CONDITIONS ARE IMPORTANT TO ACHIEVE GOOD RESULTS.

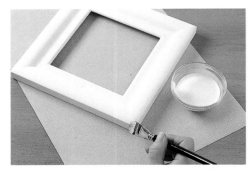

1 Using the flat sable paintbrush, apply four coats of white gouache paint to the frame, allowing each coat to dry for 5–10 minutes before applying the next. Once the gouache is dry, gently sand all around the frame using fine-grade sandpaper. Spray the frame with clear spray lacquer to make the surface less absorbent.

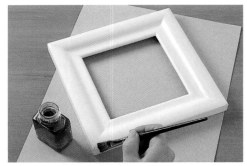

2 Using the flat oil paintbrush, apply a coat of antiquing varnish sparingly over the frame and leave for 3 hours. The longer you leave the antiquing varnish to dry, the smaller the cracks will be.

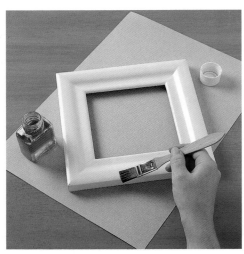

3 When the varnish is slightly tacky, apply the craquelure glaze. Cracks will begin to appear in an hour or so, depending on the temperature of the room. It is best to leave the frame to dry overnight before continuing on to the next stage.

4 Once the cracks have appeared and the varnish is dry, place some olive green oil paint on a plate. Cover your index finger with a cloth and dip it into the oil paint. Apply the paint to the frame in strokes, working the colour into the cracks, until the frame is covered.

5 Continue around the frame, wiping the oil paint off with the cloth. This will remove the paint from the surface but leave the colour in the cracks.

MATERIALS AND EQUIPMENT YOU WILL NEED
2.5 CM (1 IN) FLAT SABLE PAINTBRUSH • WHITE GOUACHE PAINT • PREPARED AND SANDED FRAME • FINE-GRADE SANDPAPER • CLEAR SPRAY LACQUER •
2.5 CM (1 IN) FLAT OIL PAINTBRUSH • CRAQUELURE VARNISH • OLIVE GREEN OIL PAINT • PLATE • CLOTH

# SCORCHED FRAME

THIS TECHNIQUE INVOLVES BURNING A DESIGN INTO THE WOOD ON THE FACE OR SIDES OF THE FRAME, OR BOTH, WITH A HEATGUN. A CLOSE-GRAINED WOOD SUCH AS RAMIN IS RECOMMENDED; THE MORE OPEN-GRAINED THE WOOD, THE GREATER THE CHANCE OF THE DESIGN SPREADING AND BLURRING. IT IS BEST TO USE A SIMPLE, FAIRLY LARGE DESIGN. A METAL FOIL TEMPLATE IS USED HERE, IN THE SAME WAY THAT YOU WOULD USE A CARD (CARDBOARD) TEMPLATE.

1 Draw your design on metal foil using a white chinagraph pencil. Cut out the design with a craft knife or wire cutters. Place your metal template on to the bare frame. Using the heatgun and wearing safety gloves, scorch the design into the wood, holding the heatgun 10–15 cm (4–6 in) away from the wood.

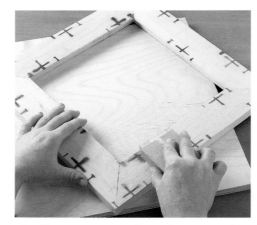

2 Using coarse-grade sandpaper, sand off the over-burns. Repeat with fine-grade sandpaper.

3 Mix raw sienna pigment with clear wax in the proportion of 1.5 ml (¼ tsp) of pigment to 15 ml (1 tbsp) of clear wax.

4 Apply the pigmented wax to the frame with a soft cloth. Work all around the frame.

5 Using a dry, clean cloth, polish up the wax to a soft sheen.

MATERIALS AND EQUIPMENT YOU WILL NEED

METAL FOIL • WHITE CHINAGRAPH PENCIL • CRAFT KNIFE OR WIRE CUTTERS • JOINED AND SANDED ASH OR OAK FRAME • HEATGUN • SAFETY GLOVES • COARSE-AND FINE-GRADE SANDPAPER • RAW SIENNA PIGMENT • CLEAR WAX • SOFT CLOTHS

# RAISED MOTIF FRAME

THREE-DIMENSIONAL PATTERNS APPLIED ON THE FACE OF A PICTURE FRAME ARE SIMPLE TO CREATE WITH ORDINARY INTERIOR FILLER. THE FILLER CAN BE TINTED ANY COLOUR YOU CHOOSE BY ADDING EITHER PIGMENT, GOUACHE OR WATERCOLOUR PAINT AND BLENDING IT IN THOROUGHLY. ALTERNATIVELY, YOU CAN COAT THE ENTIRE FRAME WITH FILLER TO ACHIEVE A PLASTER-LIKE EFFECT, AND THEN PLACE RAISED DESIGNS ON TOP.

1 In a glass bowl, combine the cobalt blue gouache paint with water in the ratio of 1 part gouache to 3 parts water. Blend in well. Apply this wash on to the frame with the paintbrush in long, even strokes from mitre join to mitre join. Leave to dry for approximately 15 minutes.

2 Lightly distress the face and edges of the frame by rubbing with fine-grade sandpaper all over.

3 Trace a design for the frame using the template at the back of the book, then transfer on to stencil card (card stock). Place this on a cutting mat and cut out the design with a craft knife.

4 Mix interior filler with water in the ratio of 2 parts filler to 1 part water to achieve an ice cream consistency. Add paint or pigment to tint the filler. Place the stencil template on to the frame and hold it securely. Apply the filler with a stencil brush in a stippling motion.

5 Leave the interior filler to dry for approximately 30 minutes, then lightly sand with fine-grade sandpaper.

MATERIALS AND EQUIPMENT YOU WILL NEED

GLASS BOWLS • COBALT BLUE GOUACHE PAINT • JOINED AND SANDED FRAME • 2.5 CM (1 IN) FLAT SABLE PAINTBRUSH • FINE-GRADE SANDPAPER • TRACING PAPER • PENCIL • STENCIL CARD (CARD STOCK) • CUTTING MAT • CRAFT KNIFE • INTERIOR FILLER • PIGMENT • STENCIL BRUSH

# FRAMED STONE

BIRCH PLYWOOD IS USED IN THIS UNUSUAL FRAME BECAUSE OF ITS STRENGTH. THE HEAVIER THE STONE YOU WISH TO FRAME, THE THICKER THE PLYWOOD NEEDS TO BE. FOR A HEAVY STONE, YOU WILL ALSO NEED TO REPLACE THE GALVANIZED NAILS WITH STRONG SCREWS. USE THE FRAME TO DISPLAY A SLAB OF STONE CARVED WITH A HAMMER AND CHISEL, AS HERE, OR ALTERNATIVELY PAINTED OR SCRATCHED WITH A DESIGN. WHEN YOU ARE HANGING A WEIGHTY PIECE OF ARTWORK SUCH AS THIS, IT IS ADVISABLE TO USE STRAP HANGERS AND TO HANG IT DIRECTLY FROM SCREWS IN THE WALL, NOT ON WIRE OR CORD.

1 Measure and saw the birch plywood to fit the stone, allowing for a border approximately 4 cm (1½ in) all round. Using a drill with a masonry bit, drill four holes in the stone, one in each corner.

2 Sand the plywood first with coarse, then fine-grade sandpaper, using a cork sanding block to smooth it down. Wearing latex gloves, apply olive green oil paint with a soft cloth all over the plywood. Rub it well into the plywood. Buff with a clean, soft cloth.

3 Place the stone on to the plywood and level up. Place a cloth over the galvanized nails to avoid marking the stone when you hammer in through the drilled holes.

## MATERIALS AND EQUIPMENT YOU WILL NEED

TAPE MEASURE • TENON SAW • 18 MM (¾ IN) BIRCH PLYWOOD • DRILL • MASONRY BIT • COARSE AND FINE-GRADE SANDPAPER •
CORK SANDING BLOCK • LATEX GLOVES • OLIVE GREEN OIL PAINT • SOFT CLOTHS • 2.5 CM (1 IN) GALVANIZED NAILS • TACK HAMMER

# METAL FOIL FRAME

THIS ATTRACTIVE FRAME INCORPORATES TWO METAL FOILS, ONE COPPER AND ONE BRASS. YOU CAN ALSO USE OTHER METAL FOILS, SUCH AS ALUMINIUM OR ZINC. WORKING WITH METAL FOIL GIVES PLENTY OF OPPORTUNITY FOR EXPERIMENTATION: SHAPES CAN BE CUT OUT AND SCORED ON THE REVERSE SIDE OF THE FOIL, FOR EXAMPLE, TO GIVE AN EMBOSSED APPEARANCE ON THE FRONT OF THE METAL. THE METAL FOIL IS QUITE EASY TO CUT OUT USING A CRAFT KNIFE.

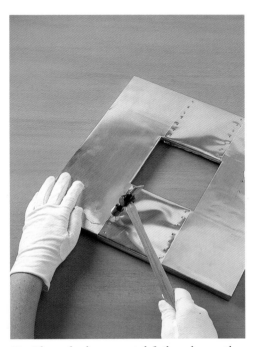

**1** Cut out a piece of copper foil (or pieces, as shown here) to fit over the frame, allowing for overlaps around the inner rebate and outer edge. Place the frame face down on the foil. Score the foil with a ballpoint pen around the inner rebate and outer edge. Remove the frame. Using a straight edge and craft knife, cut out the corners on the outer edge in line with the score marks. Cut the inner rebate window and mitre the corners.

**2** Fold the inner rebate foil around the moulding (see diagram). Tack it on to the frame with small brass pins, after making the initial holes with a bradawl. Repeat on the outer edge. Place a brass pin in all four corners, where the foil will overlap.

**3** Place the brass metal foil underneath the frame and fold it over, after making initial holes with the bradawl, then pin. Hammer pins at the edges of the brass foil to create the design. ▶

fold foil around
inner rebate

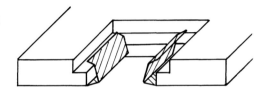

## MATERIALS AND EQUIPMENT YOU WILL NEED
THIN SHEET OF COPPER FOIL • SCISSORS OR WIRE CUTTERS • PREPARED FRAME • BALLPOINT PEN • STRAIGHT EDGE • CRAFT KNIFE • CUTTING MAT • TACK HAMMER • BRASS ESCUTCHEON PINS • BRADAWL • BRASS METAL FOIL • WIRE (STEEL) WOOL • PROTECTIVE GLOVES • STENCIL CARD (CARD STOCK) OR ALUMINIUM METAL FOIL • BLACK FELT • WHITE CHINAGRAPH PENCIL • FABRIC GLUE AND BRUSH

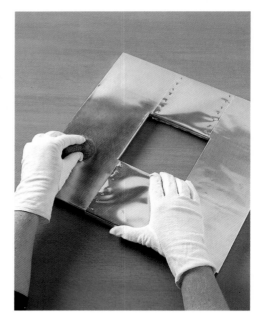

4 Using wire (steel) wool and wearing protective gloves, score the copper foil in small circular motions.

5 Cut out a template using stencil card (card stock) or aluminium foil. Place the template on the brass foil. Using wire wool, make small circular motions on the brass foil to score it.

6 Using a craft knife, cut out a piece of black felt to cover the back and edges of the frame, which are sharp. Mark an opening for the window with a white chinagraph pencil, then cut it out with a craft knife.

7 Coat the back of the frame with fabric glue, then place the piece of black felt on the glue.

8 Fold the edges of the felt into the back of the window, taking care not to overlap it on to the rebate.

# DECOUPAGE FRAME

THE ART OF PAPER DECORATION HAS EXISTED SINCE ANCIENT TIMES IN MANY CULTURES, NOTABLY IN CHINA, JAPAN AND POLAND, AND IT REACHED A HIGH POINT IN EIGHTEENTH-CENTURY EUROPE. THE WORD "DECOUPAGE" COMES FROM THE FRENCH "DÉCOUPER", MEANING "TO CUT UP", AND IT IS A TECHNIQUE USING PAPER CUT-OUTS TO CREATE SCENES AND DESIGNS ON FURNITURE, WALLS, SCREENS AND OTHER ARTICLES. THE PAPER CUT-OUTS ARE PAINTED, PASTED ON AND THEN SEALED WITH SEVERAL COATS OF LACQUER, WHICH MAKES THESE PAPER DECORATIONS VERY HARDWEARING.

1 Using the 2.5 cm (1 in) flat sable paintbrush, apply acrylic gesso over the prepared frame. Allow to dry, then apply another four coats of gesso, allowing each coat to dry before applying the next. Once the acrylic gesso is completely dry, sand it down gently with fine-grade sandpaper wrapped around a sanding block. Do not wet the sandpaper.

2 Combine 1.5 ml (¼ tsp) of yellow ochre pigment with 30 ml (2 tbsp) of water and blend thoroughly until there are no flecks of pigment in the mixture. Using the flat sable paintbrush, apply two coats of the yellow ochre pigment mixture over the frame. Allow to dry.

3 Photocopy the designs you wish to use from a book or magazine. Place the photocopies on a cutting mat and carefully cut out the shapes with a craft knife, cutting along the outside edge of each design. ▶

MATERIALS AND EQUIPMENT YOU WILL NEED •

2.5 CM (1 IN) FLAT SABLE PAINTBRUSH • ACRYLIC GESSO • JOINED AND SANDED FRAME • FINE AND COARSE-GRADE SANDPAPER •
CORK SANDING BLOCK • YELLOW OCHRE PIGMENT • PHOTOCOPIED DESIGNS • CUTTING MAT • CRAFT KNIFE • NO 2 ROUND SABLE PAINTBRUSH •
WATERCOLOUR PAINTS • PVA (WHITE) GLUE • SPRAY LACQUER • 2.5 CM (1 IN) LACQUER PAINTBRUSH • SHELLAC • WHITE SPIRIT (ALCOHOL) •
WET-AND-DRY PAPER • SOFT CLOTHS • METAL POLISH

4 Using the no 2 round sable paintbrush, paint the photocopies with watercolour paints.

6 Once the glue is dry, apply a coat of car spray lacquer over the cut-outs. This will stop the painted photocopies bleeding into the coloured frame.

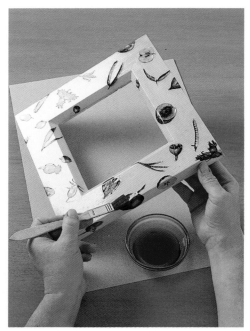

7 When the lacquer is dry, use the lacquer brush to apply successive layers of shellac to the frame, allowing each coat to dry before applying the next. When the paper photocopies are buried below the shellac, you have applied enough; usually ten coats will be sufficient. Once the shellac is completely dry, rub the frame down with white spirit (alcohol). Use wet-and-dry paper and the cork sanding block if the frame is flat, then use a finer wet-and-dry paper. Wipe off excess white spirit with a dry cloth. Apply a small, pea-sized amount of metal polish on to a cloth and polish all around the frame. Buff up the frame with a clean, dry cloth to finish.

5 Glue the photocopied cut-outs to the frame with PVA (white) glue. Press them down carefully to remove air bubbles.

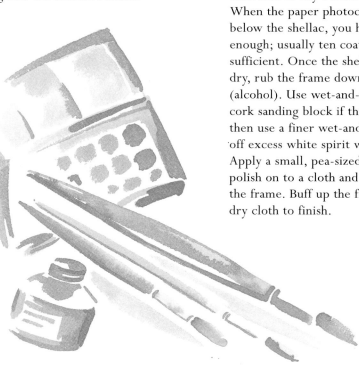

# LEAD FRAME

THIS HIGHLY UNUSUAL FRAME IS VERY STRIKING AND ALLOWS YOU TO SEE ALL OF THE FRAMED OBJECT, IN THIS CASE A FEATHER. IT IS ADVISABLE TO USE THIS FRAMING METHOD ONLY FOR SMALL OR LIGHTWEIGHT OBJECTS AS WITH TIME THE SELF-ADHESIVE LEAD TENDS TO MOVE. FOR A MORE DECORATIVE EFFECT, GILD THE GLASS AS IN THE *VERRE EGLOMISÉ* PROJECT, DISTRESSING THE GOLD (OR SILVER) LEAF SO THAT THE FRAMED OBJECT IS VISIBLE.

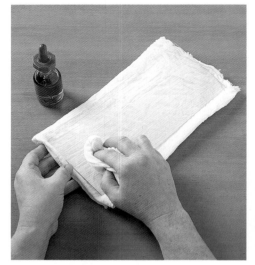

1 You will need two identically-sized pieces of glass that have been cut following the method described in Basic Techniques. Clean the glass thoroughly with a cloth dipped in methylated spirits (turpentine).

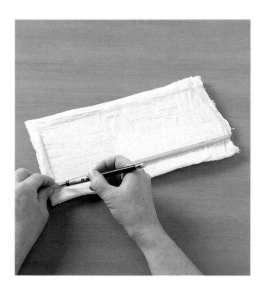

2 Measure the wood fillets against the sides of one piece of glass and mark with a pencil where they are to be cut.

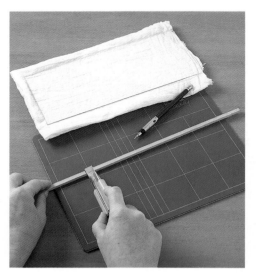

3 Once the fillets have been measured and marked, cut along the pencil line with a craft knife on a cutting mat. Alternatively, use a hacksaw with a thin blade.

## MATERIALS AND EQUIPMENT YOU WILL NEED

GLASS • CLOTH • METHYLATED SPIRITS (TURPENTINE) • 5 MM (¼ IN) THICK FILLETS • PENCIL • CRAFT KNIFE • HACKSAW (OPTIONAL) • CUTTING MAT • THICK BLACK MARKER PEN • EPOXY RESIN • BRADAWL • NYLON THREAD • FEATHER OR OTHER LIGHTWEIGHT OBJECT • PROTECTIVE GLOVES • SCISSORS (OPTIONAL) • SELF-ADHESIVE LEAD • PLASTIC TOOL • SELF-ADHESIVE HANGERS

**4** Colour the fillets all over with a thick black marker pen and put aside.

**6** Using a bradawl, make a small hole in the remaining fillet and pass a length of nylon thread through it. Secure this.

**8** Place the feather in the frame and stick the remaining top fillet to the glass. Place small drops of epoxy resin on to all four fillets then place the second piece of glass on top. Leave to set for approximately 10–15 minutes, preferably with a weight on top.

**5** Using epoxy resin, stick the blackened fillets on three sides of one piece of glass, leaving the top section open.

**7** On the other end of the nylon thread, stick the feather with epoxy resin.

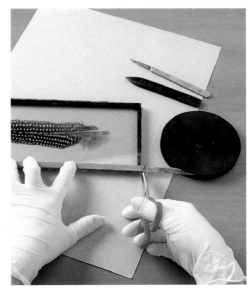

**9** Wearing protective gloves and using scissors or a craft knife, cut self-adhesive lead strips to the size of the glass edges, just overlapping the edge. ▶

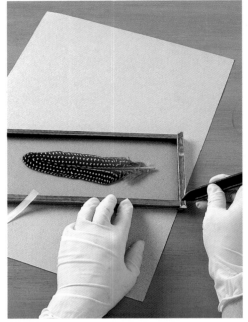

**10** Warm the lead strip in the palm of your hand for a few seconds (which will make the glue on the self-adhesive lead become more tacky). Remove the backing strip, place the lead strip on to the frame edges and apply pressure with a plastic tool. Trim off the excess using a craft knife. Continue all around the frame. Place self-adhesive hangers on to the back of the frame to complete.

# OIL-GILDED FRAME

GILDING IS A TRADITIONAL TECHNIQUE WHICH LOOKS MAGNIFICENT ON MANY WOODEN SURFACES. PATIENCE IS REQUIRED WHEN HANDLING GOLD LEAF FOR THE FIRST TIME BUT THE RESULTS ARE DEFINITELY WORTHWHILE. IN THIS FRAME 23¾ CARAT ITALIAN GOLD LEAF WAS USED ON BOTH THE FRAME AND THE GLASS, LINKING THE TWO TOGETHER VERY EFFECTIVELY. IN SPITE OF THE DELICACY OF THE GOLD LEAF, THIS FORM OF GILDING IS EXTREMELY HARDWEARING.

**1** Paint the frame with several coats of ultramarine gouache, allowing each coat to dry completely before adding the next. Draw a design on the frame with a white chinagraph pencil.

**2** Using a no 2 oil paintbrush, apply the oil size to the marked design. Leave the size to dry for 15–20 minutes. It should then be slightly tacky.

**3** Place the gold leaf on to the gilder's cushion. Cut it into squares of the appropriate size with a gilder's knife.

**4** Brush the gilder's tip on your hand or the side of your face, then pick up the gold leaf with the tip.

**5** Carefully place it on the oil-sized design. Leave to dry for another 20 minutes, then gently press the gold leaf down with cotton wool (cotton balls).

**6** After 15–20 minutes, gently wipe off the excess gold leaf with a no 4 round sable paintbrush or a small pad of cotton wool.

## MATERIALS AND EQUIPMENT YOU WILL NEED

PAINTBRUSH • ULTRAMARINE GOUACHE PAINT • FRAME • WHITE CHINAGRAPH PENCIL • NO 2 ROUND OIL PAINTBRUSH •
OIL SIZE (½ HOUR DRYING TIME) • GOLD LEAF (LOOSE) • GILDER'S CUSHION • GILDER'S KNIFE • GILDER'S TIP •
COTTON WOOL (COTTON BALLS) • NO 4 ROUND SABLE PAINTBRUSH

# VERRE EGLOMISÉ MIRROR

*VERRE EGLOMISÉ* IS GLASS THAT HAS BEEN DECORATED USING GOLD OR SILVER LEAF. THE TECHNIQUE IS NAMED AFTER AN EIGHTEENTH-CENTURY ART DEALER, JEAN-BAPTISTE GLOMY, WHO SPECIALIZED IN GILDED GLASS, BUT THE TECHNIQUE DATES BACK TO THE ROMANS.

1 Using the paintbrush and wearing latex gloves, apply the metal polish to the frame. Dab the sponge over the polish as you work along the frame for a textured finish. Leave for 30 minutes. Apply a second layer of metal polish, again sponging as you work along the frame. Leave overnight to dry thoroughly.

2 Apply a coat of black patina over the frame, wiping it off as you work. The patina will remain in the recessed areas, giving the impression of age.

3 Leave the frame to dry overnight then polish the entire frame with a burnishing tool for a soft sheen.

4 To make the mirror: clean the glass thoroughly to remove all dirt and grease, using a cloth dipped in methylated spirits.

5 Place half a gelatine capsule in a glass bowl and add a little boiling water. When the capsule has completely dissolved, add 300 ml (½ pint / 1¼ cups) cold water.

6 Place the glass at an angle of 45 degrees in a tray, so that the solution can run down freely. Cut the gold leaf into small squares. Using a 2.5 cm (1 in) flat sable paintbrush, apply the solution to the glass then immediately place the gold leaf on the solution using the gilder's tip. ▶

## MATERIALS AND EQUIPMENT YOU WILL NEED

2.5 CM (1 IN) FLAT OIL PAINTBRUSH • LATEX GLOVES • METAL POLISH • JOINED AND SANDED FRAME • SPONGE • BLACK PATINA •
BURNISHING TOOL • GLASS • CLOTHS • METHYLATED SPIRITS • GELATINE CAPSULES • GLASS BOWL • DEEP TRAY • GILDER'S KNIFE •
WHITE GOLD LEAF (LOOSE) • GILDER'S CUSHION • GILDER'S TIP • 2.5 CM (1 IN) FLAT SABLE PAINTBRUSH • KETTLE • COTTON WOOL
(COTTON BALLS) • PUMICE POWDER (0003 GRADE) • SAFETY MASK • BLACK LACQUER SPRAY

**7** Work from the top to the bottom of the glass. Continue until you have gilded the entire glass, then leave to dry. When the gold leaf is shiny, it is dry. If it is matt, it is not yet dry.

**9** Once completely dry, gently brush off any excess gold leaf with a pad of cotton wool (cotton balls).

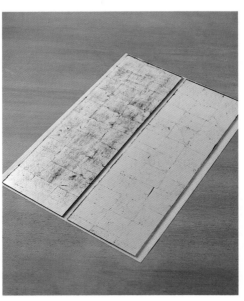

**11** When the desired effect is achieved, brush away the excess pumice powder.

**8** To seal the leaf, hold the gilded glass approximately 20–25 cm (8–10 in) away from the steam from a boiling kettle. Leave to dry once more.

**10** A more distressed, antiqued look is achieved by gently rubbing pumice powder with your fingertips into the white gold leaf. Rub it in using fairly straight strokes.

**12** Wearing a mask and latex gloves, spray black lacquer over the ungilded side of the glass. Hold the spray about 20–25 cm (8–10 in) away for an even coat. Leave to dry.

# FRAMING A CANVAS

IN THIS TYPE OF FRAME, THE ARTWORK IS NOT PLACED BEHIND A REBATE BUT INSTEAD SITS FLUSH WITH THE FACE OF THE FRAME. A GAP SURROUNDS THE CANVAS, WHICH GIVES IT DEPTH; THE WIDTH OF THE GAP DEPENDS ON PERSONAL PREFERENCE. IT IS NOT CUSTOMARY TO GLAZE OIL PAINTINGS AS THEY ARE FAIRLY ROBUST AND USUALLY HAVE A PROTECTIVE LAYER OF VARNISH. HERE THE FRAME IS COLOURWASHED TO MATCH THE COLOURS IN THE PAINTING.

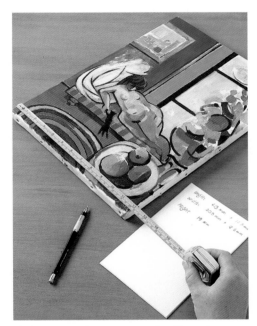

1 Measure the canvas and add on 5 mm (¼ in) to the vertical and horizontal measurements. This will give a gap around the canvas when it is eventually inserted into the frame. Measure the depth of the canvas and choose a moulding that is deep enough to allow the canvas to lie flush with the face of the frame.

2 Mix 2 parts ultramarine gouache with 1 part ivory black gouache in a glass bowl. Blend together and add 4 parts water. Mix well with a 2.5 cm (1 in) flat sable paintbrush. This is a very opaque solution. Apply the wash in long, smooth strokes on the face and then the side edges of the frame. Leave to dry for 30 minutes.

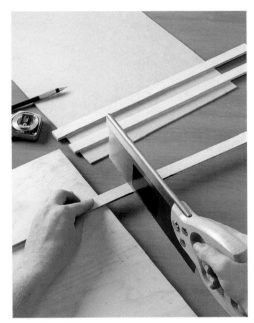

3 Turn the frame face down on to a piece of cloth, avoiding damage to the face of the frame. Measure the inside vertical and horizontal edges of the frame. These measurements are for the fillets and the hardboard. Following these measurements, mark and saw the fillets to fit inside the rebate of the frame. ▶

MATERIALS AND EQUIPMENT YOU WILL NEED

TAPE MEASURE • CANVAS • JOINED AND SANDED FRAME • ULTRAMARINE GOUACHE PAINT • IVORY BLACK GOUACHE PAINT •
2.5 CM (1 IN) FLAT SABLE PAINTBRUSH • GLASS BOWL • CLOTH • PENCIL • FILLETS, 2.5 CM (1 IN) WIDE, 5 MM (¼ IN) DEEP • TENON SAW •
HARDBOARD • BLACK EMULSION (LATEX) PAINT • PVA (WHITE) GLUE • BRADAWL • 1 CM (½ IN) SCREWS • SCREWDRIVER • FRAMER'S PIN GUN OR
PANEL PINS AND TACK HAMMER • SELF-ADHESIVE BACKING TAPE • CRAFT KNIFE

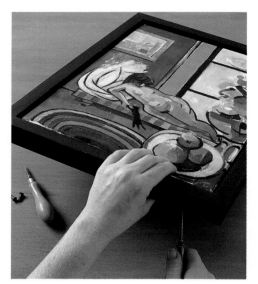

4 Using black emulsion (latex), paint one face and edge of all the fillets and approximately 5 cm (2 in) on the edge of the face of the hardboard. Leave to dry. Paint the edge of the canvas.

6 When the fillets are secure, place the hardboard, painted side facing inward, on to the frame and pin into position, using a framer's pin gun, or alternatively use panel pins and a tack hammer.

7 Place the canvas into the front of the frame, lining it up so it is straight. Holding the canvas in position, make a hole in the back of the frame through the hardboard. Insert a screw and screw down with a screwdriver, ensuring that the screw penetrates the wooden batten of the canvas. Repeat in all four corners.

5 Once the fillets have dried, apply PVA (white) glue on to the unpainted side of each one and place them into the frame.

8 Tape up the back of the frame, covering the pins. Cut mitres in the backing tape, where the tape covers both the moulding and the hardboard.

# FRAMING A TEXTILE

WHEN FRAMING A TEXTILE IT IS ADVISABLE TO AVOID USING ANY FORM OF ADHESIVE AS THIS WILL EVENTUALLY DAMAGE THE TEXTILE IRREVERSIBLY. THE BEST THREADS TO USE ARE CLEAR NYLON THREAD OR, BEST OF ALL, ACID-FREE CONSERVATION COTTON. THE METHOD OF DECORATION USED ON THE FRAME IS A WONDERFULLY SIMPLE TECHNIQUE, ACHIEVING THE LOOK OF HAND LETTERING. ANY PHOTOCOPIES, FROM LETTERING TO PICTURES, MAY BE USED.

**1** Sand the frame first with medium-, then with fine-grade sandpaper. This will produce a smooth finish.

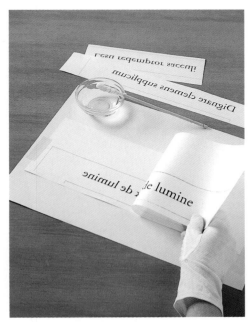

**2** Cut the photocopies into strips and place them face down on plain paper, securing with masking tape. Wearing gloves, apply a small amount of silkscreen cleaner on to a piece of cotton wool (cotton balls) or a cloth. Gently wipe this on to the reverse of the photocopy. Then, using a dry piece of cotton wool or a cloth, wipe over the photocopy again. This will transfer the photocopied text on to the plain paper in reverse.

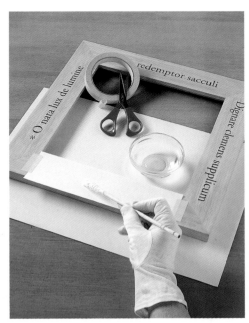

**3** Place the reversed photocopy evenly on to the frame and secure with masking tape. Using a small amount of silkscreen cleaner on a swab, gently apply this on to the photocopy. Then, using dry cotton wool, gently wipe over the photocopy. Remove the applied photocopy and leave the frame to dry for 10 minutes. ▶

## MATERIALS AND EQUIPMENT YOU WILL NEED

FRAME • MEDIUM- AND FINE-GRADE SANDPAPER • PHOTOCOPIES • SCISSORS • PLAIN PAPER • MASKING TAPE • LATEX GLOVES • SILKSCREEN CLEANER • COTTON WOOL (COTTON BALLS) OR SOFT CLOTH • CAR SPRAY LACQUER • SAFETY MASK • MOUNT BOARD OR BARRIER BOARD • CRAFT KNIFE • CUTTING MAT • RULER OR STRAIGHT EDGE • TEXTILE • PENCIL • SEWING NEEDLE • ERASER • NYLON THREAD

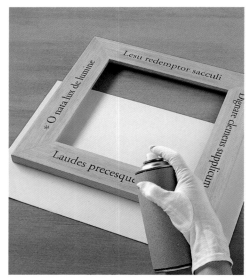

**4** Continue transferring lettering all around the frame in this way until completed. Wearing a safety mask, apply a coat of car spray lacquer, holding the can approximately 20–25 cm (8–10 in) away. This will seal the applied lettering.

**6** Make pinpricks with a needle in the board, then erase the pencil marks.

**7** Thread the needle with nylon thread and sew the textile on to the board. Do not sew too tightly as this may pull and stretch the fabric. A stronger needle may be required when sewing on to mount board, as it is thicker than barrier board. A leather needle is good for this purpose.

**5** Cut out a piece of mount board or barrier board 2.5 cm (1 in) larger all round than the textile. Lay the textile on to the board and mark with the pencil where to sew the securing stitches.

**8** To finish, pull the nylon thread through to the back of the board and secure in place with masking tape.

# BIRCH PLYWOOD FRAME

PLYWOOD IS A CONSTRUCTION MATERIAL CONSISTING OF THIN SHEETS OF WOOD GLUED TOGETHER. THE GRAINS OF WOOD IN ADJACENT SHEETS ARE ARRANGED AT RIGHT ANGLES TO EACH OTHER, WHICH MAKES PLYWOOD EXCEPTIONALLY STRONG FOR ITS LIGHT WEIGHT. WHEN SANDED AND ROUNDED OFF, PLYWOOD MAKES AN UNUSUAL AND PLEASING PATTERN. FINISH THE FRAME WITH DANISH OIL FOR A DRAMATIC THREE-DIMENSIONAL EFFECT.

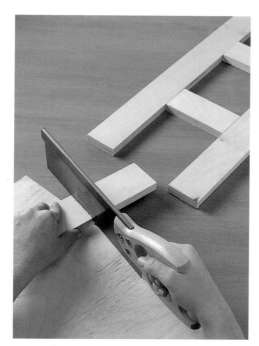

1 With a tape measure and pencil, mark the lengths and widths of the plywood and saw the pieces to length. Butt the plywood pieces together to check that they fit well. Cut the back of the frame and set aside. Sand down all the edges.

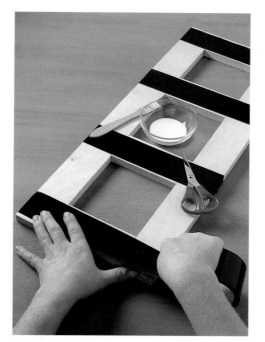

2 Apply PVA (white) glue to the side edges of the horizontals and strap gaffer tape around the frame, both front and back. Wipe off excess glue with a damp cloth and leave overnight to set.

3 Once the PVA glue has set, remove the tape. Using the cork block and coarse-grade sandpaper, sand the face and all edges of the frame. This will reveal the dark and light layers of wood within the ply. For a smooth finish, sand again with fine-grade sandpaper. ▶

## MATERIALS AND EQUIPMENT YOU WILL NEED

18 MM (¾ IN) BIRCH PLYWOOD: 2 FRONT VERTICALS, 60 x 6 CM (24 x 2½ IN); 4 FRONT HORIZONTALS, 13 x 7 CM (5 x 2¾ IN); BACK, 60 x 25 CM (24 x 10 IN) • TAPE MEASURE • PENCIL • TENON SAW • PVA (WHITE) GLUE AND BRUSH • GAFFER TAPE • SCISSORS • CLOTHS • CORK SANDING BLOCK • COARSE-AND FINE-GRADE SANDPAPER • DANISH WOOD OIL • LATEX GLOVES • FABRIC • RULER • CRAFT KNIFE • HEAVY WEIGHTS OR G-CLAMPS • TACK HAMMER • 2.5 CM (1 IN) LARGE-HEADED NAILS • EPOXY RESIN

**4** Place some Danish wood oil in a dish. Wearing latex gloves, apply the oil over the wood in a circular motion using a soft cloth. Work the oil well into the wood. Buff up with a clean soft cloth.

**5** On the back part of the frame that will face the front, apply a line of PVA glue, approximately 3 cm (1¼ in) in from the edge. Stick the fabric on to it.

**6** Once the glue has set, trim off excess fabric using a ruler and craft knife.

**7** Apply PVA glue on to the back of the front section, then place this section on to the fabric-covered section.

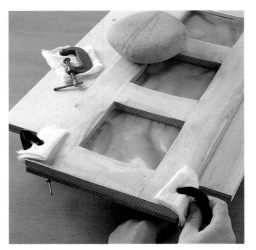

**8** Place heavy weights or G-clamps on all four corners and the middle section. Wipe away excess glue with a damp cloth and leave to set overnight. Place a cloth below the weights or clamps to prevent damage to the face of the frame.

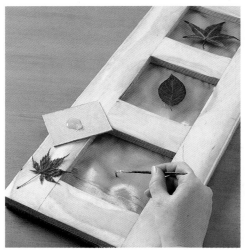

**9** When the glue has set, apply a coat of oil on the side edges of the back section of the frame. Mark out the centre of each window and hammer in a large-headed nail, leaving approximately 1 cm (½ in) showing. Mix a small amount of epoxy resin and apply this to the nail heads. Place the object on top and leave to set.

# RECLAIMED TIMBER FRAME

RECLAIMED TIMBER HAS A NATURAL DISTRESSED AND HEAVY APPEARANCE, AND IS ONE OF THE EASIEST FRAMES TO CONSTRUCT. ITS AMPLE DEPTH ALLOWS FOR PLENTY OF CREATIVE THREE-DIMENSIONAL EFFECTS. THIS FRAME REQUIRES NO FINISH, RELYING INSTEAD ON ITS NATURAL CHARACTERISTICS FOR ITS RUGGED APPEAL. AS WITH ANY HEAVY FRAME, IT IS ADVISABLE TO USE STRAP HANGERS AND TO HANG IT DIRECTLY ON TO SCREWS PLACED IN THE WALL.

1 Measure and mark with a pencil the length and width of the verticals and horizontals. Saw with the tenon saw to the correct sizes. Lightly sand the sawn edges.

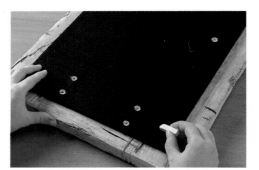

2 Cut the hardboard to size. On one side apply fabric glue, then stick down a piece of black felt on top. On the other side stick down a piece of decorative paper. Mark out corner holes for the screws, using chalk.

3 Turn the cut lengths of timber face down and butt them together at the corners. Place the felt-covered hardboard on the back of the timber. Make initial holes in the hardboard with a bradawl, then screw into the back of the frame, making sure that the frame remains still. The screws will hold the frame together.

4 Turn the frame the right way up and nail in the corner brackets, using galvanized nails.

5 Cut small fillets to size, coat with PVA (white) glue, then place below the framed object to give a three-dimensional effect.

## MATERIALS AND EQUIPMENT YOU WILL NEED

RECLAIMED TIMBER: 2 VERTICALS 62 x 10 CM (25 x 4 IN); 2 HORIZONTALS, 18 x 10 CM (7 x 4 IN) • TAPE MEASURE • PENCIL • TENON SAW • SANDPAPER • 54 x 28 CM (22 x 11 IN) HARDBOARD • FABRIC GLUE • BLACK FELT • DECORATIVE PAPER • CHALK • BRADAWL • 14 x 2.5 CM (1 IN) SCREWS • SCREWDRIVER • 4 RECLAIMED BRACKETS • 8 x GALVANIZED 2.5 CM (1 IN) NAILS • HAMMER • 5 MM (¼ IN) DEEP FILLETS • PVA (WHITE) GLUE AND BRUSH • NATURAL OBJECT FOR FRAMING

# PENWORK FRAME

Penwork was one of many artistic amusements popular at the end of the eighteenth century. Its inspiration comes from India and it imitates the craft of ivory carving where the design was wiped over with black pigmented wax, which remained in the recesses of the carving while the surface of the ivory remained white. This elegant black-and-white cassetta frame is created by painting the frame solid white, using gesso to cover the bare wood, then transferring a traced design on to it in black ink.

**1** Brush acrylic gesso in long strokes along the entire frame, first the face section and then the edge. Allow to dry for approximately 20 minutes, then repeat. A minimum of four coats of gesso is required. Sand the gesso with medium-, then fine-grade sandpaper to achieve a smooth surface. Apply four layers of white acrylic paint over the frame, allowing each coat to dry for approximately 5–10 minutes before applying the next.

**2** Place tracing paper over your design and trace with a 2B (#2) pencil or use the templates at the back of the book. If necessary, place masking tape on the tracing paper to hold it steady.

**3** Place the tracing, pencil-side down, on the frame, and secure with masking tape. Using a 4H (#4) pencil, draw over the design. This will transfer the pencil design on to the frame.

**4** Remove the tracing paper and ink over the design with a fine black marker pen. Paint the rebate with black emulsion (latex paint) or ink it in.

**5** When the penwork is completed, wear a safety mask and spray clear lacquer over the frame to seal, holding the can approximately 20–25 cm (8–10 in) away. Leave to dry for 5–10 minutes. One coat of lacquer will be sufficient.

**6** Using a flat lacquer brush, apply four layers of shellac over the frame, allowing each coat to dry for about 30 minutes before applying the next. This will give an aged ivory appearance.

MATERIALS AND EQUIPMENT YOU WILL NEED

PAINTBRUSH • ACRYLIC GESSO • JOINED AND SANDED FRAME • MEDIUM- AND FINE-GRADE SANDPAPER • WHITE ACRYLIC PAINT •
TRACING PAPER • DESIGN (TEMPLATE) • 2B (#2) PENCIL • MASKING TAPE • 4H (#4) PENCIL • FINE BLACK MARKER PEN •
BLACK EMULSION (LATEX) PAINT • SAFETY MASK • CLEAR LACQUER SPRAY • 2.5 CM (1 IN) FLAT LACQUER BRUSH • SHELLAC

# TORTOISESHELL FRAME

Tortoiseshell was extremely popular in the eighteenth century, particularly on hairbrush sets, trinket boxes and small frames. Manufactured plastic tortoiseshell is readily available nowadays, but it tends to look plastic. This method of creating the look of tortoiseshell is fairly realistic, using pigments suspended in shellac. A little time, perseverance and patience are required.

**1** Apply yellow ochre oil paint all over the frame, and leave to dry overnight. Apply another coat and allow to dry overnight again.

**2** Apply oil size over the face and outer edges of the frame using the flat oil brush. Leave to dry for 15 minutes. When slightly tacky, begin to apply the gold leaf.

**3** Place the gold leaf on the gilder's cushion and cut it into appropriate-sized squares or rectangles, using the gilder's knife. Brush the gilder's tip on the side of your face to enable it to pick up the gold leaf. Place the tip gently on the gold leaf and pick it up vertically. Place the gold leaf gently on the oil-sized sections of the frame, without letting the tip touch the frame, then lift the tip up vertically. Repeat all round the frame, until it is completely gilded.

## MATERIALS AND EQUIPMENT YOU WILL NEED

Yellow ochre oil paint • 2.5 cm (1 in) flat oil paintbrush • Joined and sanded frame • Oil size (½ hour drying time) •
Gold leaf • Gilder's cushion • Gilder's knife • Gilder's tip • Cotton wool (cotton balls) • Shellac •
2.5 cm (1 in) lacquer paintbrush • Pigments: yellow ochre, burnt sienna, Venetian red, burnt umber •
No 2 round sable paintbrush • White spirit (alcohol) • Fine-grade sandpaper • Cloths • Metal polish

**4** Once the frame is gilded all over, let it dry for 20 minutes. Gently tamp down the gold leaf with a pad of cotton wool (cotton ball). Leave overnight.

**5** Using the lacquer brush, apply four layers of pure shellac over the frame, allowing each layer to dry for 30 minutes before applying the next.

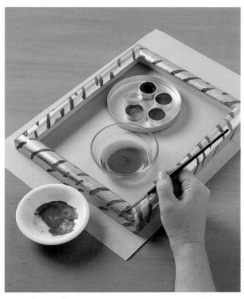

**6** On a small plate mix 30 ml (2 tbsp) of shellac with 1.5 ml (¼ tsp) of yellow ochre pigment, using a no 2 round sable paintbrush. Paint this mixture on to the frame diagonally, leaving gaps for the rest of the pigments.

**7** Repeat step 5. Then repeat step 6, replacing yellow ochre pigment with burnt sienna.

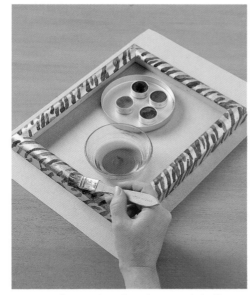

**8** Apply another four layers of shellac, allowing each to dry for 30 minutes before applying the next.

**9** Repeat step 6 with Venetian red pigment. Apply four layers of shellac, allowing each coat to dry completely before applying the next.  ▶

**10** Repeat step 6, using the burnt umber pigment.

**11** Apply eight layers of shellac, allowing each layer to dry completely before applying the next. Leave overnight.

**12** When the shellac is touch dry, dip fine-grade wet-and-dry sandpaper into a bowl of white spirit (alcohol) and very gently sand all around the frame, ensuring that the sandpaper is saturated with white spirit. Be careful not to sand through to the pigmented layers.

**13** Wipe off excess white spirit with a cloth. Then apply a small amount of metal polish and polish with another cloth. This should produce a smooth and shiny finish.

**14** Polish the entire frame with a fresh clean cloth.

# EMILY'S FRAME

For this project, a fairly wide-faced and deep moulding is required due to the oblongs and squares that will be chiselled out. This frame is very unusual and has scope for a wide range of creativity. It is decorated with natural objects, including slate pebbles which are ideal as they are flat. If you require an opaque effect, decorate the glass following the instructions in the *Verre Eglomisé* Frame project. Because the decoration is so complex, the artwork is the frame itself so use it to frame either a strong or simple image.

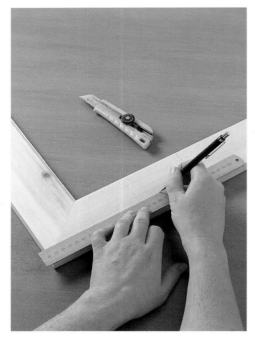

1 Mark out oblongs and squares on the face of the frame with a ruler and a soft pencil. Do not place the shapes too close to the rebate or the outside edge.

2 Score the pencil marks on the frame with a craft knife and a ruler.

3 Chisel out the squares. Remember to chisel fairly deeply, so that the glass will not protrude from the face of the frame.

## MATERIALS AND EQUIPMENT YOU WILL NEED

JOINED FRAME • RULER • SOFT PENCIL • CRAFT KNIFE • CHISEL • CORK SANDING BLOCK • COARSE- AND FINE-GRADE SANDPAPER •
2 MM THICK GLASS • GLASS CUTTER • T-SQUARE • SOFT CLOTH • LATEX GLOVES • OLIVE GREEN OIL PAINT • ETCHING SPRAY • MASKING TAPE •
PROTECTIVE MASK • BLACK CARD (CARDBOARD) • CUTTING MAT • PVA (WHITE) GLUE AND BRUSH • SLATE PEBBLES AND OTHER DECORATIVE
OBJECTS • WHITE CHINAGRAPH PENCIL • EPOXY RESIN

4 When all the squares have been chiselled out, sand the entire frame with the cork sanding block and coarse-grade sandpaper, then repeat the sanding with fine-grade sandpaper.

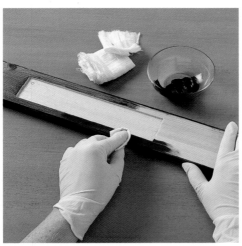

6 Using a soft cloth and wearing latex gloves, apply the olive green oil paint over the frame, working it well in.

7 Decorate the glass with *verre eglomisé* for an opaque effect. Spray some of the glass with a little etching spray so the objects underneath are still visible. To decorate the glass for the slate pebbles, place masking tape in two strips over the glass and spray on the etching spray in a line down the centre, holding it approximately 20 cm (8 in) away and wearing a protective mask. When dry, remove the tape.

5 Cut all the glass to the sizes required using a glass cutter and a T-square.

8 Cut a piece of black card (cardboard) for the background, apply PVA (white) glue and insert into the chiselled-out space. Mark and cut out card fillets to the appropriate size. ▶

**9** Glue the fillets into the chiselled oblong with PVA glue.

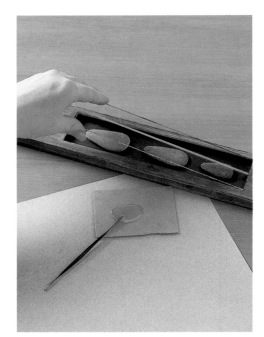

**11** Glue the glass on to the fillets using epoxy resin.

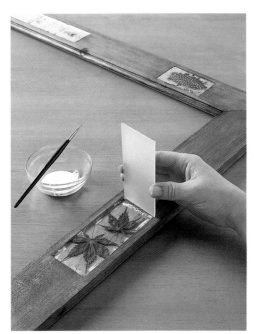

**12** Add other decorative elements to the frame as desired. If the objects are flat and small, glue them in the glass with PVA glue, which will dry transparent.

**10** Glue the slate pebbles on to the black card background using epoxy resin.

# TEMPLATES

PENWORK FRAME pp84–85 (NOT SCALED)

RAISED MOTIF FRAME pp54–55 (NOT SCALED)

# SUPPLIERS & ACKNOWLEDGEMENTS

**AUTHOR'S ACKNOWLEDGEMENTS**
Many thanks and lots of love go
to the following wonderful
people: Andrew Jakeman for his
exceptional patience, Paul
Jakeman for supplying copious
amounts of tea, Robert Randall
for just putting up with me,
Doreen for her guidance, Nicki
for her styling and photography,
Leonard Villa and Jennifer
Dinsmore for their valuable
knowledge. Special thanks to
Ben for many slices of toast and
for the use of his computer.

**SUPPLIERS**
The publishers would like to
thank the following for supplying
equipment for photography:

L. Cornellisen & Son Ltd
105 Great Russell Street
London WC1B 3RY
Tel: 0171 636 1045

Crown Fasteners and
    Fixings Ltd
Watermill House
Restmor Way
Hackridge
Surrey SM6 7AH
Tel: 0181 773 3993

Frame Factory
20 Cross Street
London N1
Tel: 0171 226 6266

Hobbs & Co
88 Blackfriars Road
London SE1 8HA
Tel: 0171 928 1891

Leonard Villa Framemakers
    and Gilders
316 Caledonian Road
London N1
Tel: 0171 700 5010

Metal Paint Ltd
PO Box 80
Hitchin SG5 1FF
Tel: 01462 451451

E Ploton (Sundries) Ltd
273 Archway Road
London N6
Tel: 0181 348 0315

Rose and Hollis
G8 Belgravia Works

159–163 Marlborough Road
London N19 4NS
Tel: 0171 272 5551

Robert Randall, Woodcarver
14 St. John's Road
London N19

Alec Tiranti
27 Warren Street
London W1P 5DG
Tel: 0171 636 8565
*and*
70 High Street
Theale
Reading RG7 5AR
Tel: 01189 302775

**PICTURE CREDITS**
The publishers would like to
thank the following agencies
for permission to reproduce
pictures in this book:

Page 8, Jean-Loup Chaumet
(top right, bottom left),
e. t. archive (bottom right);
page 9, Bridgeman Art Library,
(bottom left and top right),
e. t. archive (centre); page 10,
e. t. archive (top), Jean-Loup
Chaumet (bottom centre),
Bridgeman Art Library (bottom
right); page 11, Bridgeman Art
Library (top), Jean-Loup
Chaumet (bottom).

# INDEX

Adam brothers, 9, 11
anti-theft devices (ATDs), 32
assembling frames, 27–9

backing tape, 28–9
Baroque style, 9
barrier boards, 27
birch plywood:
    birch plywood frame, 79–81
    framed stone, 56–7
book mounts, 23
Bosch, Hieronymus, 8
brass foil, metal foil frame,
    58–60
Brustolon, Andrea, 9
builders' moulding, 30
butterflies, 27–8, 32

canvases, framing, 73–5
cleaning glass, 27, 29
colour, stepped window
    mounts, 36–7
colourwashed frame, 46–7
composition frames, 10–11

copper foil, metal foil frame,
    58–60
cord, 28, 32
cow hitch knot, 28
craquelure frame, 50–1
cutting:
    frames, 24–5
    glass, 26–7
    mounts, 22–3

decorative window mount,
    34–5
decoupage frame, 61–3
D-rings, 27–8, 32

Emily's frame, 90–3
Empire frames, 10

equipment, 20–1
etching spray, 18, 91

fabrics, velvet-covered mount,
    38–40

filler, raised motif frame, 54–5
"fitting up", 27–9
fixings, 32
float mounts, 23
foil, metal foil frame, 58–60
frames:
    birch plywood frame, 79–81
    for canvases, 73–5
    colourwashed frame, 46–7
    craquelure frame, 50–1
    decoupage frame, 61–3
    Emily's frame, 90–3
    framed stone, 56–7
    lead frame, 64–7
    lime-waxed frame, 44–5
    metal foil frame, 58–60
    oil-gilded frame, 68–9
    penwork frame, 84–5
    raised motif frame, 54–5
    reclaimed timber frame,
        82–3
    scorched frame, 52–3
    for textiles, 76–8
    tortoiseshell frame, 86–9
    woodstained frame, 48–9
François, Maître, 8

gesso, penwork frame, 84–5
gilding:
    oil-gilded frame, 68–9
    tortoiseshell frame, 86–9
glass:
    cleaning, 27, 29
    cutting, 26–7
Glomy, Jean-Baptiste, 71
gluing frames, 25

gold leaf:
    oil-gilded frame, 68–9
    tortoiseshell frame, 86–9
    verre eglomisé mirror, 70–2

hanging pictures, 33
heatguns, scorched frame,
    52–3
history, 8–11

joining frames, 24–5

knots, 28

lacquer:
    decoupage frame, 61–3
    penwork frame, 84–5
    tortoiseshell frame, 86–9
lay-on mounts, 23, 29
lead frame, 64–7
lettering, framing a textile,
    76–8
lime-waxed frame, 44–5

materials, 18–19
measuring pictures, 22
metal foil frame, 58–60
mirror plates, 32
mirror, verre eglomisé, 70–2
mitre boxes, 24
mitre clamps, 24
mouldings, 30–1
mounts:
    cutting, 22–3
    decorative window mount,
        34–5
    measuring, 22
    multiple window mount,
        41–3
    order of fitting up, 29
    stepped window mount,
        36–7

types of, 23
    velvet-covered mount, 38–40
multiple window mount, 41–3

Neo-Classicism, 10, 11

oil-gilded frame, 68–9
overhand knot, 28

paints, colourwashed frame,
    46–7
panel pins, 28
paper, decoupage frame, 61–3
penwork frame, 84–5
picture cord, 28, 32
picture frame moulding, 30
pin guns, 28
plywood:
    birch plywood frame, 79–81
    framed stone, 56–7

raised motif frame, 54–5
Randall, Robert, 16
reclaimed timber frame, 82–3
Renaissance, 9, 10
Rococo style, 9, 11

Sands, Ashley, 17
scorched frame, 52–3
shellac:
    decoupage frame, 61–3
    penwork frame, 84–5
    tortoiseshell frame, 86–9
single window mounts, 23
slate, Emily's frame, 90–3
spring clips, 32
stepped window mount, 36–7
stone, framed, 56–7
strap hangers, 32

tabernacle frames, 9
techniques, 22–33

templates, 94
Teniers, David II, 10
textiles, framing, 76–8
tortoiseshell frame, 86–9
triptychs, 8, 41

ultra-violet light, 33
underpins, 25

varnish, craquelure frame,
    50–1
velvet-covered mount, 38–40
verre eglomisé mirror, 70–2
Villa, Leonard, 14, 16

wax:
    colourwashed frame, 46–7
    lime-waxed frame, 44–5
window mounts:
    decorative window mount,
        34–5
    multiple window mount,
        41–3
    order of fitting up, 29
    stepped window mount,
        36–7
    velvet-covered mount, 38–40
wire, 32
wood:
    mouldings, 30–1
    reclaimed timber frame,
        82–3
woodfiller, 25
woodstained frame, 48–9

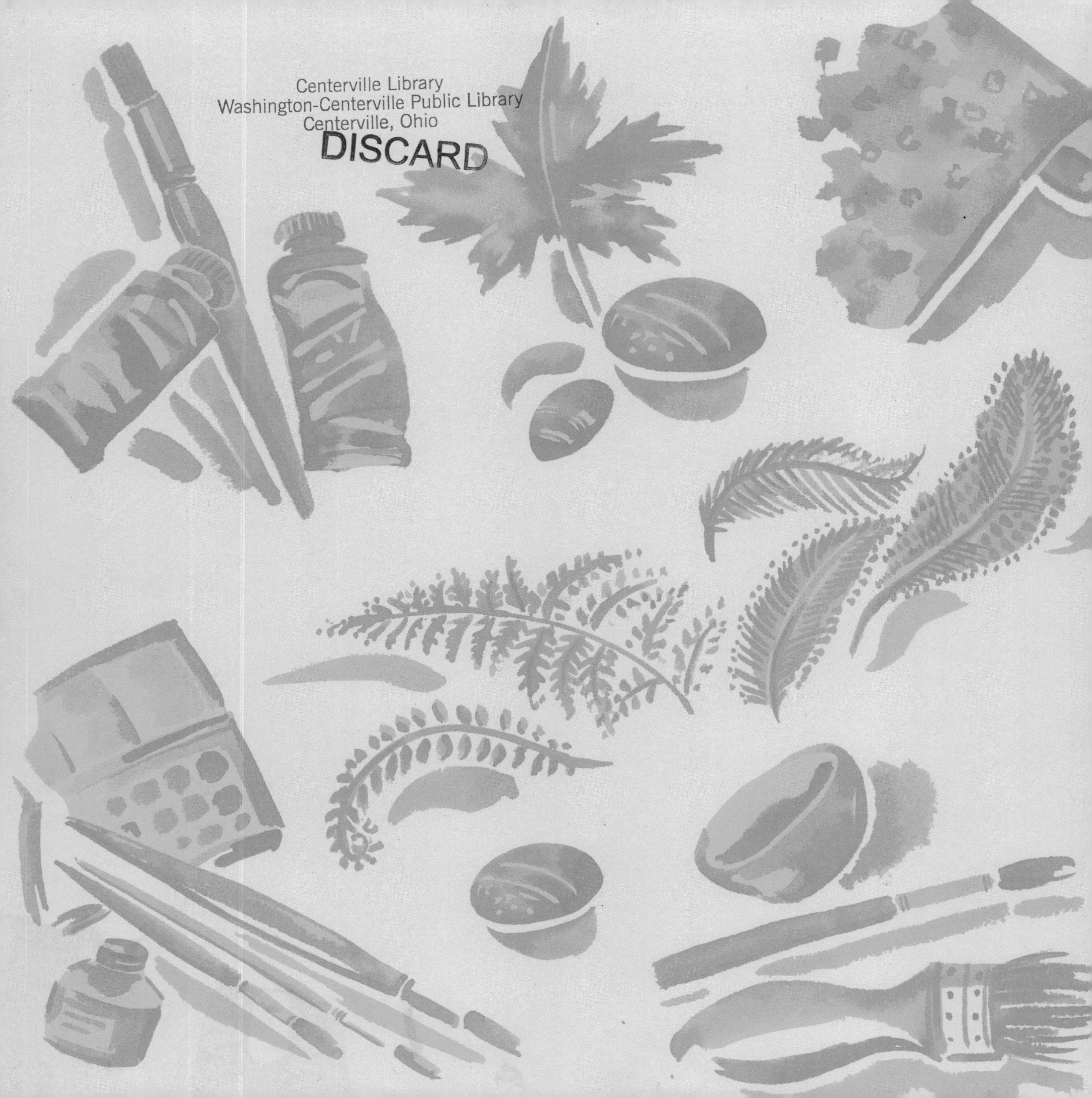